HUNGER MOON

Poems

Susan Deer Cloud

Hunger Moon

ISBN: 978-0-9853151-7-7
Library of Congress Control Number: 2014931365

Cover art by Dorothy Little Sparrow Watson

Published by Shabda Press
Pasadena, CA 91107
www.shabdapress.com

(I dwell here
As the muskrat dwells in the waters at the bottom of the hill
Life for life's own sake,
Simple as the falling snow,
Trying not to think too hard
About the hardships that are sure to come)

Evan T. Pritchard, Mi'kmac

HUNGER MOON is especially dedicated to …

John Gunther who brought me home to the Catskill Mountains

Meaghan Palmer, great niece who knows about courage & transformation

Dorothy Little Sparrow, beloved Cherokee friend and cover artist

Preface

We are living during an age of immense upheaval, economic and emotional depression, and transitions we dream will bear us into a happier time for our blue planet. I am one little person walking Taoist-like across the high peaks and deep valleys of this chaotic landscape. Yet despite the increasing economic divisions in America, the "forever war," being spied on, and Mother Earth being ill-used and overpopulated to a shocking degree, I have much beauty and love in my "flash of a firefly" existence. I hope that light shimmers through in this book I chose to call *Hunger Moon*. I have never believed in "making nice" or "playing to the pretty" the way so many women have been pressured to do from girlhood through womanhood. Instead, I bear witness to those who stridently insist we are "being victims" whenever we speak out against the so-called "one percent" oppressing us. If we protest the hardships and misery of other people's lives, the smug money mongers accuse us of making excuses for those who have no excuse for being jobless, poor, ill-nourished, bereft of home and hope.

Here is what I find inexcusable ... kicking people when they are down and desperate, afraid and unbearably sad. I remain free enough not to be brainwashed into being willfully cruel. I remember every single person who kicked me when I was already hunched on a bare apartment floor, sobbing. And I recall every human being who extended a warm and understanding hand to me. Happily, I have a vast circle of friends/family who refuse to cave in to the herd animal instinct of conforming to *au courant* mean-spiritedness and cynicism. I agree with Tennessee Williams' Blanche DuBois that the "one unforgivable sin is deliberate cruelty." This is one way I refuse to be a victim ... by not being deliberately cruel.

I have experienced more than one Hunger Moon in my life while also tasting many seasons of fullness in the ancient heart ways. I feel enduring gratitude to all the good people who are a part of the poems in this book ... to those who have shored me up when I did not know if I could stay strong enough to even continue living. If I started naming them one by one, I would have another book! I grew up in relative solitude in an upstate New York town, so how wonderful to be graced by a constellation of star friends. Stars, I hope you see where you are blazing herein.

I especially want to thank those Turtle Island visionaries who gave me such eloquent blurbs for my book ... Evan T. Pritchard, Barbara Alice Mann, Paul Hapenny and Anecia Tretikoff O'Carroll. I am over-joyed that Cherokee Dorothy Little Sparrow did the front cover and that my sister, Erelene Clear Deer, took the photograph of me dancing barefooted in snow on my 60th birthday. Yes, I hold to "a rebirth of wonder." In the spirit of such wonder, I marvel that my traveling com-panion, John Gunther, has borne me back to live in my home country, the Catskill Mountains, full circle to the very street where I was born. Lastly, how thrilling that the brilliant writer, Teresa Mei Chuc, is editor and publisher of *Hunger Moon*. There shimmers a Red Thread between us that no one and no thing can ever sever. Nya'weh.

Susan Deer Cloud 1.25.2014

Acknowledgments

Adrienne Rich, a Tribute Anthology – "Door"

I Was Indian II Anthology – "Uphill"

Mo'Joe Anthology – "Chief Joe"

Syracuse Y Downtown *Writers Center Anthology* – "Rides High Horses," "Long Dirt Nap"

Turn Up the Volume: Poems on the States of Wisconsin – "Peaceful Assembly"

http://beaverkillfriends.org/writers.html – "Swims with Frogs," "Shy Bird," "Quieter Times in Their Hands"

Binghamton Press & Sun-Bulletin – "The Gingrich Who Stole Christmas"

Chiron Review – "Rainbow Sister"

CounterPunch, reprinted in *LaBloga* – "Reading the Names"

CounterPunch – "It's Easy When You Love an Indian in Prison"

Earth's Daughters – "Ritual" & "Baloney"

Glass – "Marbles"

Naugatuck River Review – "The Winter Women"

Oddball Magazine – "Martin Luther King, Jr. Night," "When It Snows, Women Hold Quieter Times in Their Hands"

Paterson Literary Review – "Hunger," "Verticals," "When the Puerto Ricans Came to Town"

Pluck! Lost Ones Issue – "Black Hoodie"

SERVAS Newsletter – "Surprising Gift"

Stone Canoe – "The Pen Factory," "Crossing Over Mid-Hudson Bridge"

Stone Soup *Spoonful Journal* – "One Night, Two Poets"

Talking Stick – "All April Day It Rained"

The Mas Tequila Review – "How to Get Hired as an Indian Professor"

To Topos/Poetry International – "Red Lake"

Winning Writers website 2007 – "Ice Storm"

Without Halos – "Violin"

Yellow Medicine Review – "Back to the Blanket," "On Turtle's Back Rising," "Zen Board for a Beloved Warrior," "A Winter Poem of Making Love," "Snow Sculptor, Snow Moon Dream," "This Jesus Cat"

Contents

Part I

Crying for a Vision, Snowstorm

I suppose you want my poems to be
about dancing in feathers at powwows

or hiking up to some generic
purple majesty mountaintop out West,

fasting on long freezing nights and
crying for a vision. Here is the vision

I am crying for in my dump of a freezing
apartment in Binghamton, New York ...

enough to cover rent plus cable television
so my cat and I can watch our nature shows

loud enough to block out the gunshots
on this street the city plows last.

Verticals

Florida February, Collier-Seminole Park's
Pioneer-Indian Days ... and you strolling past
booths of dream catchers, feathered dance fans,
beaded earrings, flutes waiting for the dreamer's
breath. No evidence of pretend pioneers,
only real Indians greeting you. We chat, smile,
share stories, feel as though we are the People
who won. At booths' end a wheeled cage,
a sleeping Florida panther inside the verticals
of black bars. Ever since you first flew south
you have longed to be this close to Panther,
find one lone one opening its gleaming eyes to you
in the flowering wilds along the sea ... one
to replace the glow-eyed felines slaughtered
to extinction in Catskills where you come from.

Still, you are accustomed to how wishes
get granted in ways not wished. The non-Indian
in cowboy hat displaying the panther is pleasant,
eager to educate. You ask questions about
these Florida wild cats, indicate your willingness
to be educated about trapped beasts. Listening,
you stare beyond bars at pure feline sleeping inside
a shadow-universe. Fur same color as hot beach.
Eyes shut to sand. Your sun-burnt hand stretches
towards panther belly rising, falling, as in deepest
dream back to day your Indian grandfather took you
to Binghamton's Ross Park Zoo. Outside lion cage,
ignoring sign warning you not to disturb the lions
asleep behind verticals of bars, your grandfather
roared, roaring long, loud, wild ... roaring until
the lions woke, roaring to his roars, making
your small bones shake.

You have read how neuroscientists experimented
on small-boned kittens during the 'Sixties.
Columbus-like, those torturers discovered
if they raised a kitten with one eye sewn shut,
it would always view life with a blind eye
even when the cruel thread was cut.
And when a kitten was walled inside
a world of horizontals it could never see up-
and-down lines, nor could kittens visually
suckled by verticals know anything
but bars. You regard the other Indians
in their booths, consider how hard
it has been for Natives to see past
glowing eyes once sewn shut, past
the horizontals of tragic history,
the verticals of private hurt,
just to smile in the sun. It is hard
to not return to what's trapped
inside bars. In his cowboy hat
the keeper of wild cats is still talking.
Your hand that yearned to touch
the panther slumps back on your heart
that silently roars as Grandfather roared
the day he woke the sleeping lions.

How to Tell the Difference Between an Indian and a Native American

An Indian always goes by the name *Indian*. Even with college degrees,
publications, prestigious awards and, of course, still no job, an Indian
won't answer to *Native American* (which explains the "no job" part).
Some Indians, though, find work in Hollywood, thanks to Coyote
who enjoys a good belly laugh. An Indian speaks softly, means
any politeness. The Indian differs from the Native American because
you can piss a Native American off and they'll keep right on smiling.
A Native American fears being stereotyped as *savage*, although
Native Americans secretly relish being dubbed *noble*.
An Indian can feel afraid, even terrified, but won't continue
smiling if pushed too hard. Usually this takes awhile.
Think King Philip, Chief Tiyanoga, Sitting Bull, Crazy Horse,
Winona LaDuke, Barbara Mann, Paula Gunn Allen and Deer Cloud.

A Native American thinks that because of federal recognition,
casinos, dollars piling up and an increased ability to leap
with two feet clad in Gucci sneakers over to the white man's boat,
things are looking up. An Indian knows better. Consider Indians
who "off" themselves. Read Amnesty International statistics ...
more Indian women in the U.S. get raped than other women.
Any Indian knows if you pack a concealed heart, vast and verdant
as the stolen land ancestors dwelled free on, there will be nights
of grief. Not just Chief Joseph "I will fight no more forever" grief,
but "I will smile no more forever" black bear-lumbering depression.
Wooden Indian isn't a stereotype. Some Indians' hearts are cut
by wooden splinters into puzzle pieces that will never fit
other pieces to make a pretty picture. Too many lost pieces.

The Native American and Indian are not always easy to tell apart.
It's not like the days when the Indian was the one with moccasins,
beads, buckskin clothes, pride and prayers woven through braids.
Here is something that takes a long time ... the centuries it requires
to get on the other side of a person's skin. This Indian doesn't care

what anyone says. Crawl to the underside of a Native American's skin,
you'll find a player who's already dead. Gallop to the far country
of an Indian's skin, no matter how broke, broken, beaten, scarred,
you will be drawn to touch there tenderly that which doesn't lie,
that which yet lives. No language exists to explain this odd survival
of red deer, mountain laurel, stars flaming in night rivers, scarlet
tanagers, surprise of gold eagles in the high, clean places.
It's like trying to explain love.

And the final difference between a Native American
and an Indian? The Native American will force Love
to sit, beg, roll over before flinging it a gnawed wishbone.
The Indian understands what starvation is. An Indian
will treat Love as a panther, free magnificence,
yellow-eyed mystery, there to feed song to, poetry to,
laughter to, give one's heart flaming with night stars
to. An Indian remembers what it feels like to wander
in a forest after the panthers are pronounced extinct.
If you walk side-by-side with the loneliness of an animal
disappeared forever, then you will know that last
difference. You will know the way an Indian loves.
And you will love forever.

Shy Bird

In first winter storm
a bird much like a snowbird
flashes to feeder
feathers mottled white and grey

A field of wild snow her hair

Lift up camera
surprise of bird flies away
in air wings unnamed
in mist mountains disappear

A shawl of shyness her skin

Catskill Hillbilly Indian

In 1950s we were called "part Indian."
We ourselves filled in the blanks
with the non-Indian parts like puzzle
pieces. I grew up in a stucco house
my Mohawk grandfather built next
to one he built for him and Grandma.
Behind the house an old mill race,
beyond its paradise of frogs the forest …
in front, just across School Street,
the school I entered when I was four.

My teacher, Miss Church, was like
her name, expecting us to do all her
blond divinity bid us to … walk in single
file, take naps each day, not stray into
the berry bushes when she marched us
in snake formation out to the playground.
I made friends with another "part Indian"
who sneaked into the bushes with me.
We "played Indian," plotting how to scalp
teacher and gallop away on wild ponies.

But no ponies in those sheltering bushes,
so we "snuck" back out whenever
Miss Church blew her whistle
for making another line in my little
life that had been all circles up to then.
Speaking of "snuck," teacher didn't wish us
to say that word or "ain't," "git," "fit,"
"brag upon" and "chimbly." Any hillbilly
who kept dropping hard "g's" in "lookin',"
"singin'," "rainin'," etc., would *get* spanked.

Weird thing was, I wanted Miss Church
to like me. But I seen her grammatical face
suspecting I only spelled trouble.
She fawned over a doctor's niece,
girl who had the halo hair of angels,
eyes like sun-filled sky. My eyes
smoldered pine-green and at first
I cried myself to sleep at night
because now I knowed I talked bad
and dark hair and freckles weren't purty.

Away from school, I remained encircled
by the softening speech of Catskills,
expressions and lilts from centuries-old
English lit by candles and hearth fires.
Soon I corrected Mommy and Daddy
on their way of breeze-soft talkin'.
What shame my heart carries for growing
ashamed of them. How scairt when they said,
"You must do good in school, graduate
college so you won't end up like us."

Before Columbus Day, then Thanksgiving,
Miss Church taught us about the savage Indians.
I grew civilized enough not to say "Thanksgivin"
or call Columbus and the Pilgrims "Indian killers."
I wore my mother's hand sewn dresses strewn
with docile flowers, learned to raise my hand
to speak, use fingers to color inside prison bar lines.
Teacher gave me "G's" on my report card. "G"
for Good. "G" for Girl pinning g's on words
like kicked dogs with drooping tails.

Violin

Another artifact preserved by women, this violin,
curved like a woman's body in its broken case,
scratched wood weightless as some wounded
bird on torn velvet, violet-red.
Late winter, when her mother died,
she carried the instrument from its case again,
cradled it like a found child on her childless thighs.
Snapped strings shot out from a dark bridge, star-
silver, bridging her own dark times
and that barb-wired night when
her grandmother's favorite brother died, sunk
in Second World War mud trenches.

A memory, not even her own ...
a mad dreamer fiddling mountain tunes
in a French farm field,
knee-deep in murdered boys.
She lifts the bow, at its frayed end
mother-of-pearl, touches the violin
returned home from that far violence,
her great-uncle's stilled hands.
Since then, silent music of women
passing down violin past repair,
from daughter to daughter, hand
to dreaming hand.

Deer Meat

No one in our Catskills called it venison
anymore than mountain people said
"pasta" for spaghetti. My family
were such people, Indians
whose ancestors fled from somewhere far,
from the soldiers, the bounty hunters,
from concentration camps called reservations.

The Indians married in with Catskill
Scotch Irish, English, etc., while the forests
became both longhouse and cabin,
sky starry tepee and bell tower.

And so I think of first home after
my sis calls me tonight over eighty miles
of highway covering the old Indian paths,
our voices winging along Route 17
soon to be buried by I-86. For years now,
every so often she mentions Jimmy,
a "part Indian" man from our hometown.

November, we must be nearing deer season.
For six decades I've lived away, don't know
the first day for blasting buck this year.
"Remember," Pearl laughs, "the night Jimmy
showed up at our door when you came home
for Thanksgiving? All those packages
of deer meat he brought for you?"

"Fondly," I laugh back, mainly
to make her even happier. She hoots,
"Now there's a traditional Indian man for you,
courting a woman by bringing his meat to her,"
and I hear her, my mother and me

laughing until we shone after Jimmy
walked back out under the stars,

far after my mother fed the earth-eyed hunter
pumpkin pie, keeping our faces "straight"
and heating the yellow kitchen
with women's talk while Jimmy
gazed shyly at a wall or window.

When he had done eating
he picked up our little grey kitten,
slyly I followed his horse-handler hands
stroking the cat's fur soft as milkweed silk.
Maybe something lost in me purred then,
only I was a University woman
and Jimmy dwelled in the Universe
of horses, wild animals, and speaking
but a few words.

I thought of this when my sister hung up
and our laughter died in the silence
of my lonely apartment
in a dirty upstate city addicted
to ghosts. I try out my rusty "Indian way,"
being that Thanksgiving is coming,

set aside all memory of Pilgrims killing
Natives after that first Thanksgiving,
whisper in the quiet what I can be thankful for,
for instance that flannel-shirted Indian
with his last name my favorite color,
Green, new leaf green, fern green …

for one spring day when my sis and I
drove up to a mountain farm to see
the horses Jimmy was caretaker for,
when he, Pearl, and I slipped beneath

barbed wire fence and I held out a branch
of apple blossoms to the auburn colt
prancing toward us.

Jimmy spoke some then,
and I am thankful because his voice
was mountain headwaters and May breeze.
"That's a chestnut eye the colt has,
that unusual eye," he said with a soft grin.
I sing gratitude for an eye like cracked
ice over a country pond, something
too long frozen about to break
to fire then leap free,

thank you for such leaping ...
when shyly we gaze out
into the world of no words.

Bear Hunt

Granddaughter, when I crawl through
that membrane separating your life
from what people misname my death,
I can sometimes weep tears again,

as with this Hunger Moon night
when I kneel by you crumpled
under old animal hides.

Why do you curl there like a lone fiddlehead
at forest edge … or caterpillar
some stupid boy pokes a stick at?

Are you the first woman
whose husband has left with relatives
to hunt bear? Your grandfather did so.
I spent the brief days sewing bright designs
on a robe for his return.

Oh, Granddaughter, you never were a girl
who learned to embroider suns into her thoughts.

Even though your man mentioned the vast lake
he must cross over, conducted ceremony
so no thaw would come to thin its ice,

I fear you have forgotten
your bear medicine.

Why else would you nuzzle
into grief's rough fur? Why
press fists like paws
to cheekbones?

Does this make you
more real, the way
he makes you feel
when his body provides
a new skin for you?

When you become a soft green fern?
A blue butterfly in winter?

Lillie Hendrickson, Great Grandmother

I was born far back in Catskill woods
when panthers yet stretched like gold-eyed shadows
acrost high branches at night. My father was Joseph ...
his mother, Cornelia, a Mohawk medicine woman.
Whites called Papa Uncle Yope. We knew Yope
to be a bad name. Word they flung at Indians then,
same as that Southern slur that got Negroes hung.

At thirteen, a man twenty years older married me.
After the skimelton, he made me feel I warn't
a short bony girl worth nothin'. He acted like
his blue-eyed god I never see'd. We lived
in a cabin by the Willowemoc where I gave him
thirteen children. Half died, some babes, some
half grown. Typhus, scarlet fever, whoopin' cough
swallowed them up. I swallowed my tears.

Hidin' grief was all I ever studied. I couldn't
read nor write. I fished for trout, planted corn,
beans and squash, gathered nuts and berries.
I favored blue mornin' glories, growed them
by our cabin door. Heavenly blue ... closest
to any heaven an Indian girl could come.
I loved my children but daren't love them
too much in case they died. I think I was
kind enough to the ones who survived.

My husband was a carpenter who hunted
all the wild and pretty animals of the forest.
He planed my pretty body with his. By thirty
I was flattened to near bone and he called me
"old squaw." At thirty-two, ice-fishin', I crashed
through river ice, but it was pneumonia that kilt me.

My boys and girls got took to a children's "home"
in Binghamton, but it warn't no home.

Nine-year-old Harry whose cheekbones shone
like mine, blade-sharp, high as cliffs where
eagles nest, ran away. My night-haired boy
escapin' at last to our rivers, our mountains,
where his first granddaughter was October-born.
She can read and write. Her name means *lily*.
I hide behind her tree letters as we Indians hid for centuries.
Look for me in her poetry. Look deep for all our dead.

Door

Sometimes she forgot about the door
to the upstairs room she slept in
at the end of the Vietnam War.
In her small town
people left doors open.
If they shut a door, they never
locked it. Her father painted
the door delicate rose. It wasn't
what she wanted, but her mother
thought it the perfect pink
for her daughters' bedroom.

Sometimes she forgot the door
for months, a year, two years.
She forgot the teenaged girl poised
between being tomboy and woman.
Occasionally, she'd find a snapshot
from that year, her flesh in tiger-striped
bikini, glossy and tan … when boys
started to call her *Sexy*, a playmate
startled her by smiling *Your eyes are
exotic like my cat's, green with tiny suns.*

Often she forgot about the door, how
she was trained to keep family matters
shut in. It was *them* against the whole world.
It was ongoing snapshots of a family smiling
for the American Dream. But some nights
when she curls up with her exotic-eyed cat …
woman with hair chilled from autumn rain
to snow … she grows afraid, sees the lurching
shadow erase her doorway.

Usually she forgot that her brother knelt
by her bed one night when he staggered home
drunk. She fought phantoms of him in tight
briefs, huge cock poking through slit, trying
to hit him away. *Please, just a kiss,* he begged.
A sisterly kiss. Him sticking sloppy beer tongue
stinking past her lips trying to close like a door,
delicate rose. Her other drunk brother stumbled
in, dragged the first, laughing and spitting,
from the perfect room.

Often she forgot how the next day
her brother stared at her stretched
in bikini on chaise lounge in shocked
sun. He said nothing. She said nothing,
averted her face. She wondered
if her beautiful mother, so sheltered
by her father, heard any noise the night
before … but her mother only floated by
in an organdy apron and pink dress.

She thought *It can't happen again.*
But it could. Afterward, she shut
the door each night, shoved highboy
against pink, slid bureau against that.
Then she coiled shivering in heat, delicate
rose between tense thighs, cat eyes dilated
to the drunk dark, shadows threatening
to punch through door she swore
she'd not leave open anymore.

Rainbow Sister

"Pregnant!" Mommy flung her iron at Daddy's head.
I crawled behind couch, shivered in July heat
steamy as the flying iron, yanked-out cord swishing
like a sperm's tail. At seven, I'd never witnessed
my mother throw anything before. I picked
my mosquito bite scabs, bled like her red words.
"Keep picking," she used to warn, "you'll be
all scars. No man will marry you." On the surface
she showed no scars. Skin shone pearl. Only
her cheekbones, hair, hinted at the Indian "blood"
she never mentioned, the way I played dumb
when the iron that pressed my dresses into
American Dream-in-pink became a Perseid.
That day I learned how words make this world,
knowing that each night my secret tongue
had prayed for a sister.

Decades later I taste incoming falling stars
on my November tongue. Earth flings her blue
through seedings of Leonid meteorites that won't
return for another three hundred years. And
my mother? Father? Will they be as shooting stars,
spark my life and sister's life the way they did before?
That summer I was seven the GE iron my mother
used to smooth out our rumpled, mixed-blood lives
broke. Sister born at snowy midnight, 28 January.
'Sixties arrived, our lives intertwining with war,
civil protest, Day-Glo hope. "Erelene, Erelene,"
I'd chant her name that was our grandmother's name,
rock her on playground swings, sing to her as we soared
closer to Catskill mountain tops, *"The answer, my friend,
is blowin' in the wind"* blowing across Willowemoc
and trailing tractor trailers tornado-ing down
Route 17 to places my dreams ached to go.

Little Sister Erelene, you whose friends call you
Pearl as if they see how our mother's skin shone
with underwater light … today I pray for you
in another way as I float across University campus
with this knapsack of memories tattooing my back.
Today I chant for you and all like you when I behold
a sacred circle of two-spirited protestors raising
their voices against hate words spitting the "gay"
are sick, wrong, should not exist. Today I grin
in autumn sunlight, feeling a 1960's wind
blowing across the protestors' rivering hair
and rainbow faces. I remember how *we*
were forced to be silent, because we were Indian …
because we were girls … because we were poor …
were poets, were rebels … because *you* were gay.
"I'm afraid, afraid, afraid," I could hear your
whispers echo my own. Today my face marked
by my mother's tomahawk blade cheekbones
blossoms out into pearls of sound.

That summer I was seven Mommy smashed
her steam iron against living room wall. I picked
my scabs and *Who knows?* Maybe I should have
picked at them more so no man would ever
marry me. *Maybe* I should have cut my pink
dresses up into pink triangles. Erelene, I always
wondered why *you* were the gay one, not me …
both tomboys, both preferred to gallop bareback
as wild horses, preferred pants to dresses,
naked feet to shoes. We climbed high
in the apple trees … stole golden apples
instead of playing house, crayoned our dolls
in what we thought were Blackfeet war designs.

Oh, Little Sister Erelene, Pearl of my heart
blistered into sorrow at all the hate in this world,
dreaming you is what taught me how words

create this life. Oh, iris-eyed Sister and all
sisters and brothers of the rainbow, today I am
round dancing with my knapsack stuffed
with memories of silence, of how hate
can petrify anyone into a wooden Indian.
Today I offer up my prayer, again, chant
for you, for me, for us in this answering wind.

When the Puerto Ricans Came to Town

When the Puerto Ricans came to town, it was the summer
I got my first period. Breasts ached from growing so fast,
hips rounding out to accommodate the babies I swore
I'd never have. When the Puerto Ricans came to town
I was a tomboy fighting against becoming a woman.
My mother scolded me, "Stop playing basketball and baseball
with the boys. They're seeing you differently now."
When the Puerto Ricans moved to our Catskill town,
the country people glanced at them as if they landed
from another planet, glanced away as if to avoid being
beamed up to their spaceships as guinea pigs for unspeakable
experiments. When the Puerto Ricans arrived with brown skins
and curly hair and their Spanish and Spanglish and fast music
and fast mouths, people stopped treating us "part Indians"
as the only outcasts in town. We had our tomahawks
but everyone knew the "spics" packed switchblades.
When the Puerto Ricans invaded our town, their young men
with switchblade-bodies gleaming leaned against
stonewall bridge spanning the Willowemoc. Whenever
I walked to Main Street I had to take my breasts and hips
past their gauntlet of stares, trying not to sway, trying not
to jounce or smile. But whenever I walked past those
peg-legged studs so hot, so cool, as if they had just leapt
out of "West Side Story," I could feel my hips swinging
back and forth like a pendulum just marking time until
a man's hands might grasp them someday … could feel
my breasts doing the Salsa of "Yes, yes, yes." Only
my face stayed stiff and straight. When the Puerto Ricans
debuted in town, I learned more about hate the first time
a white girl married a Puerto Rican boy. And, oh, wasn't he
handsome, that boy? Everyone said so. And *she* from
the wealthiest family in town … pretty face a puzzle
of scars from when it flew through her parents' Cadillac
window one intoxicated night. But no one got as upset

over that as when her face soared so bedazzling in love
you no longer noticed the glass-reddened cheeks. Yes,
when the Puerto Ricans came the young men whistled
when I tried not to sway. They sang, "Chickie, chickie,"
while I held my head high and never answered.
But sometimes when I drive back to that small town,
saunter again over bridge where their ghosts swagger,
the jigsaw of scars inside me starts flying away
on the *chickie chickie* wings of my *grande* smile.

The Pen Factory

1969. People back then called me
a "part Indian" girl. My earliest memory ...
father's night terrors, sweats, because he'd been
shot through his chest at eighteen, my age
that crazy year of Vietnam War. A Marine,
he tried to race across Guam's coral beach
to jungle. "Can't dig a foxhole in coral,"
Dad said once. "I was totally exposed."
Oldest brothers drafted out of college,
one shipped to Vietnam, other to Korea.
I, angry young woman, dropped out of college,
spat out words like "fascist pigs," "the system"
and "1 2 3 4, we don't want your fuckin' war."
I moved in with a GWU philosophy student,
joined D.C. anti-war and civil rights marches.
Then American Indian Movement galloped in.
We formerly nice girls started to get pissed off
at the long-haired, pot-smoking, sensuous
leftists and hippies who called us "chicks."
My mother had a lung hemorrhage, so I rode
Greyhound Bus through slow miles of fall flame
back to our Catskills where she nearly died.
In the hospital she whispered
when her mouth pooled with blood
my small hand floated towards her, a vision
grabbing her hand so she wouldn't leave.
When the doctors released her, still weak,
I stayed to help out, got a job at the pen factory
where my red haired Aunt Maude worked.
We assembled pens for politicians. My body
ached on metal chair for eight hours each day,
fingers scooping up pen halves, ramming them
into second halves in whirling Army-green machine
screwing halves together. Pen after pen made

between my young flesh and inflexible machine.
The women called me "College Girl," even though
I kept my mouth shut, ate lunch with Maude
partly to protect her when the gossips tittered
the owner wanted to "fuck" my "big titted" aunt.
I believed in "power to the people," unions, labor rights,
but up close many of "the people" were cruel, spiteful,
tough. One day the rumors made my aunt cry,
when I had never seen her weep before.
I can still hear the women's coarse jokes ...
"He's that ugly because his mother threw out
the baby and kept the afterbirth" ...
"What did the Pilgrim say to the Indian
at the first Thanksgiving? *Just so you know,
this doesn't make up for all the scalpings*" ...
"What's a WOP's idea of foreplay?,"
finger snap, pointing to imaginary bed on floor ...
"What's a Jewish man's idea? *Two hours of begging*" ...
workers sniggering in Aunt Maude's direction,
wondering if Jewish owner begged her
with her fiery hair. I had read Engels, Marx,
Marcuse, watched Chaplin's "Modern Times"
at The Circle near D.C.'s Foggy Bottom,
blasted out songs from Rolling Stones'
"Beggar's Banquet," especially "Factory Girl."
What would thirty or forty years of this
do to me? How much exhaustion, hate,
resentment, roughness, could it fill me with
then empty me of so nothing was left?
My father picked Maude and me up
on the way home from his job at Berman's
Plumbing & Electric, and I didn't know it
but his war wound was catching up to him.
He'd soon be dead. We chatted about
the colors of fall leaves and going apple picking
and about my mother's growing strong enough
so we'd have a happy Thanksgiving.

Didn't mention my brothers, how they
wouldn't be with us, all of us terrified
my eldest brother would die in Nam.
Little sister hung American flag upside down
in bedroom window. Billy Bang Bang, town cop,
threatened to arrest her for it. Nights I sat near
that window, wrote with pens I snuck home
from the pen factory, the ones we workers made
for politicians, American Dream promises printed
under clear plastic. Summer of Love over,
my Turtle Island more and more soured into a jail
of lies, assassinations, the coffins of the too young.
Factory girl, shy hippie chick, Indian flower child
afraid to go pee because I might get fired, I spent
my eternities off the clock writing it all down.
Even during the "forever war," I am with those
factory workers who never spoke of liberation,
ghosts struggling to survive in the pens, pencils,
computer I use to assemble this poetry.

The Winter Women

In early 1950s the women were like the seasons,
in winter their skins paling into snow-covered
meadows, bodies snow drifts growing more still.
Gathered around our kitchen table, they smelled
of buried wildflowers, wistful as dream,

poor women married to working class men ...
my mother, her three sisters, Grandma and great aunts.
Catskill women who spoke a language of lilts and lulls,
mountains and valleys ... but when we girls started school
schoolmarms shamed us for dropping hard "g's"

until we felt ashamed of our Grannies and Mommies
always lookin' at birds flyin' in sparklin' snow
and chirpin' "How byooteefull, how byooteefull!"
through mouths daubed with lipstick a startle
of scarlet, only make-up they used.

Around red and white Formica table
the women told stories about people they knew ...
never mean gossip but a weave of tales that made
our mountain people immortal. Their laughter
rang out more holy than church bells.

In those post-War years of the great snows,
during storms the women crocheted doilies
and knitted afghans and baby clothes because
there were always newborn infants and more a comin'.
Or they would bake pies, oven-warm kitchen

swirling with cinnamon and nutmeg ...
Mother saving me a strand of dough
to sculpt into magical animals. The women
picked me up, rocked me and praised
my unicorns and panthers.

The best was the day after a blizzard
when the sun shone once more and snow higher
than I was glistened like the tiny diamond
in my mother's engagement ring, millions
and millions of diamonds blue as sky.

Part II

Hunger Moon Woman

A woman glimpsed winter full moon
through a window of a house shared
with the man she no longer recognized.
So it happens sometimes ...
one morning a person wakes up and
maybe it is that day when all the cells
in the body get replaced, or the way
a beam of light unmasks the meanness
beneath a mate's face and suddenly
he's a stranger, or a word slashes
the heart in such a way it will fight
no more forever for its once love.

So it became for the woman called
wife by the man she no longer knew.
She pulled on coat and boots and when
he was sleeping traipsed out into
the midnight of the Hunger Moon's
deep snows, feet feeling for deer paths
leading to ridge far above the house.
She hopped from hole to hole
dug by deer hoofs, snow sparked to
fire opals in fluorescent moonlight ...
through blue drifts leaping
from forest into blaze of crystals

fancy dancing across fiery field.
No need for flashlight ...
only artificial light twinkling in
distant city like upside down sky
flooding river valley. No more house
or porch bulb that first lit her way
away from the stranger. O the deer trails
beading Mother Earth, O legs lengthening

and sprouting fur, bearing her to deer
bedded down beneath pines encircling
the holy moon meadow. She knelt
and sparkled with the other deer.

Father's Day Eve

By Father's Day Eve you had moved out of
"the big house," as your husband christened it.
By Father's Day Eve you had moved into the cottage
closer to Bunn Hill Road, nearer to cars going *somewhere*,
motor sounds softening, breeze-like, on the far side
of the mountain. By Father's Day Eve you slumped
in the night on a concrete stoop, too old to get drunk.
Watching fireflies flicker green as your eyes across uncut
weeds, you saw the marriage was ended.

By Father's Day Eve, you listened to future ex-husband
whistle through a raised window up at the big house,
luring the fox, your totem animal, into artificial light.
And you thought how you were like that fox, female, hint
of fire in fur sidling through ripped shadows, exposing
yourself in order to grab, trot off, with some tossed chicken,
jam-stained bread, marshmallows flying at you, a surreal snow.

Yes, night had fallen. Beyond the fireflies and your heart's
flickering, you trotted back with your proud, glorious tail
to your summer's den of Tartarean honeysuckle, bearing
away food to carry you through tomorrow's hunger.
On Father's Day Eve you could hear the man you once loved
bang down the window after fox was gone, slam himself
in with the ghosts of your fights and tears. And there
remained the phantom of your fearful body, lingering
shimmer of flesh he no longer touched.

On Father's Day Eve you lay in secret stores
of meats and sweetness, remembering your father
in warm night air smelling like bread you baked for him.
"Let me kiss it and it'll be better," he'd say whenever
you scraped knees on Catskill sticks and stones,

freckled arms against elm bark and apple trees,
shimmying up to top branches where freedom was.

On Father's Day Eve, you remembered how it
always worked, that promise of a kiss, a cure.
Now almost all the beautiful elms were dead.
And your father dead, twenty-five years.
On Father's Day Eve you crouched on concrete,
heart scraped, bloodied, no man around. Only freedom
rising further in night sky with the tomboy moon,
moonlight kissing your silver hair.

Meaghan, the Day You Were Born

I drove from Bunn Hill Nation to Binghamton Press Building,
elevator lifting me to the ninth floor. Nine-thirty a.m., consulted
divorce lawyer for the second time. His silk suit gleamed gray
in his desk's amoral gloss. His tongue slithered, slid, glass
snakes hissing how bad it would be after the divorce. The day
you were born, Meaghan, my lawyer's face floated up
before my face like the bloated underbelly of a dead fish,
o.d.'d on excessive bottom-feeding. I yearned for home,
Catskills, native trout, even useless suckers casting slow shadows
up to river tops. But on the day you were born, Meaghan,
I only glimpsed church tops hovering, Chagall-like, in ninth-story
windows … best view evil could buy.

Meaghan, the day you were born, August 28, year 2000,
summer was ending, and I was ending. Speeding back
to my Bunn Hill cottage, I crouched in misery on rotting floor
infested with ants, rocking myself in my own arms. Day
you were born, I cried as I never had cried before. Called therapist,
got his answering service … called out to Creator, got nothing.
And, oh, Meaghan, the day you were born was hot, humid,
bodies everywhere slick with sweat. So hot, I wanted to blaze
up with fall's oncoming fire, one last flash of farewell flame,
praying I might die in winter's ice. Day you were born
afternoon seeped into twilight, darkness, some dim stars,
insects chirring their final love songs in the acrid grass.
Next door the man I once loved blasted the evening news
so loud it was as if he had remote-controlled all love songs
to mute.

Meaghan, the day you were born I lit scented candles
on my stone fireplace, breathing in honeysuckle and rose,
lilac and lavender … girlhood's lost flowerings. I knelt

in among their flames, touching my hands to hearth-rock,
touching my grandfather's Indian hands mortaring together
stone beauty of fireplaces in mountains. On the night
of the day you were born, my sister Erelene phoned.
"Tanya gave birth to a daughter this morning …
Meaghan Victoria. We are great aunts a second time."
Then … "But there's something wrong. Meaghan's
lacking part of her left jaw. Her chin sinks in to her throat.
Her left ear is a knob and may not hear. There's an asymmetry
in her tongue, two holes in her heart. Goldenhar Syndrome
is what it's called." But, Meaghan, that night of the day
you were born, my sister pronounced it "Golden Hair."

"Golden Hair." I thought of all the little girls wishing to be
pretty as Cinderella and Sleeping Beauty, 14 karat-hair dazzling
some prince into whisking them away to his castle on a hill.
On *my* hill, I remembered the time I interviewed your mother
and your Aunt Tami for a folklore course, trying to figure out
if the story "Cinderella" might wreck their brains for all eternity.
"You have blonde hair like Cinderella's," I pointed out to them.
"Oh, no," Tami said, "it's not blonde. It's *golden* hair." Across
silent miles I pleaded, "Erelene, will Meaghan be all right?,"
re-living the day your mother was born, premature …
how we weren't sure her 2.2 pounds of flesh could endure
this world. "She'll need a lot of plastic surgery,"
my sister started to cry. I wept back, "Well, you know,
the holes in the heart come from our side of the family."

I hung up the phone, Meaghan, staggered out into
the darkness, recalled how I first saw your mother held
in your grandfather's palm … love at first sight. On the night
of the day you were born I heard, again, love songs hidden
in grass. And not even seeing you in your sterile room
in a Boston hospital eight hours away, *it was love at first sight.*
"Meaghan has deep blue eyes," your great aunt Erelene
soothed me over the phone. Grand niece, in our family
we know all about "deep blue," "golden hair," "asymmetrical

tongues," and "hearts that are holy." On the day you were born, I raised my aging face to ancient night sky, found you in a star above cottage roof. And I held you, Meaghan, little Cinderella, sweeping away ash in the psalm of my heart.

The Ghost Hand

Sunrises when you opened eyes,
        stared at river stone fireplace
some former owner's dream …

After you moved into the cottage,
        built a fire in it, the rooms
billowing with phantoms of smoke …

And so placed many colored candles
        on mantle slab, hearth, where before
you placed logs, twigs, crumpled poems …

Awake in the witching hours, watching
        tiny wavering fires, your numbness
freezing into sleep …

Dawns of divorce, waking,
        not wishing to wake,
face a pond of tears …

Late April night, dead mother floating
        out of blue candle flame,
Evening of Paris perfume …

Ghost hand gathering your hand,
        touch palpable, delicate skin fire,
trying not to frighten her away …

Mother cradling writing fingers,
        chanting in candle silences,
It will be okay, you will be okay …

And she dead, *dead,* yet more alive than the living,
	long ago dreamer who led you into
the hands of the woods' emerald fire ...

Winter sunrise, opening eyes,
	O Mother, floating back to blue
chrysalis of face flying with light ...

Hunger

I was small. I was standing on the floor
in my parents' kitchen, in stucco house
my Indian grandfather built in early '50s.
It was winter but my feet were bare. I shivered
in white flannel nightgown with gold braid
my mother sewed for me for Christmas.
She said it was the gown angels wore.
Past black windows snow fell as if angels
were being torn to pieces by a violent hand.
In Sunday school they taught us about Heaven
where the angels lived. My parents promised
if I were a good girl I could live there, too.

Face pressed itself to door window …
second face behind that, breathing out
clouds. I was small. I thought angels
had come to our house, knocking, pounding,
at door, on glass. My mother opened
the door, Father beside her. "Cousin Violet,"
my mother cried, "Ted!" … before
two angels staggered into our little kitchen,
shook white off thin bodies. Their wings
were gone. "We're hungry," Violet pleaded
through cracked lips. "I know you don't have
much, but can you lend us some money?"

I was small. I peered up at Violet. I recalled
violets, purple, pretty, sometimes pressed
against poems in books. I remembered
smelling them, sucking nectar from tiny sacs
when we still had sun. "Violet," my parents
comforted the angel. "We'll give you
what you need." Husband Ted hung
his head. I was small. Shivering. Didn't

yet know about shame. Hunger. Desperation.
How to keep one's pride when the belly's empty,
when whimpering children wait back home.

I was small. Barefooted, I peered up
into Violet's eyes not looking at anything
at all. Tears thawing on gaunt cheeks.
She came from the family's Indian side,
not Heaven. No one spoke about that side,
but we all knew … we could become fallen
angels in falling snow knocking, drumming,
pounding at a door. Just yesterday
in the Giant, a young man appeared to me.
Glanced down at grapes purple as violets
in my grocery cart. "I'm hitching up north,"
he pleaded. "I'm hungry. Could you
lend me some money, *anything*, for food?"

It was snowing. Sleeting. He was young …
brown hair, patched coat glinting with melting
white. I remembered his eyes from night
when I was small. I dug through beaded bag,
found an Andrew Jackson, pressed it into
his raw hand. Knife scar on left cheekbone,
he moved his face close to mine. "Why, you have
glitter above your eyes. You're shiny like an angel."
Kissed me on my mouth. I shuddered at the years
my husband never kissed me, at bad-weather
divorce I was thumbing my way through,
dwindling bank account.

Didn't Jesus kiss Mary Magdalene on her lips,
address her as "Dearly Beloved?" Was his mouth
so soft, so thick? "It will come back to you, Love,"
stranger shoved twenty into coat pocket, strode
back out into sleet, snow. And I was small.
My mother's cousin, Violet, started to weep.

I stood crying in the Giant, falling
to kitchen floor in braided gown
my mother made for Christmas.

Shame. Pride. Torn snow falling.

Angels all around.

He Sends You "Winter Boy"

(And there'd been summer love
Love I trusted far too well, got away and winter's spell
had broke my heart and left me all alone ...
from Buffy Sainte-Marie's "Winter Boy")

He sends me a video of Buffy Sainte-Marie
singing "Winter Boy." Although
I know this favorite song will twist
free a buried anguish, I click on
Buffy's Cree tremolo and it strangles
my resurrected loss like a noose.

He sends me a memory,
doesn't realize it. Outside
last night's snow piles up
in hills made by shovels red
as blood I loosed once
into similar snows.

He calls me Mother, even though
he is as old as I. His flesh
star white as new snow glistens
into my dreams on winter nights,
and he is my babe and my lover
and I must not cry.

And my own "summer love"
a sloughed off husband who demanded
my winter boy be scraped from me ...
I could not wrench a song from that,
fly my wingless heart into a tremolo
of "gleaming" born of grief.

Instead, each midnight I trudged
across the dead fields and furious
snowdrifts so they would freeze
the place emptied ...

between thighs stop
the nor'easters of blood.

And he sends me ...

Exquisite Corpses

When the jade plant became spangled from streetlights seeping
through red blinds, it looked like a Christmas tree bringing luck.

And the earth-skinned boy opening a paisley black and white
umbrella in the middle of the street suddenly became a flower.

Jade in lamp light. Umbrella in sunlight. Indians at midnight,
on Facebook, sending words like smoke signals.

I never heard of any ancestors who sent smoke signals.
No one in my family rode horses like those rode by Indians
played by Italians and Mexicans in the old movies.

I rode a horse once at a riding stable. A boyfriend's idea
so I could recover my Blackfoot past. Black and blue for days
on the insides of my recovered wild Indian thighs.

Pictures I took of the boy. "Thank you" on yellow paper
stuck under windshield wiper after I planted a bouquet of photos
of him and his Grandma inside Grandmother Mary's door.

Desolation Row, Twilight Zone, NY. The drunks I rent from.
Every weekend rooms acrid with stench of redneck saloon
in 1950s Catskills. Beer. Gin. Cigarettes. Vomit.

Stink of violent sex. Of piss on bathroom floor.

No we won't stop smoking because you and that Korean
living next to you are allergic. We're not going to be controlled
by our tenants. Love it or leave it.

On the street, the flower boy's smile lingers above asphalt
he no longer twirls on. Boy like Buddha ... African, Asian,
Caucasian, Indian faces in one countenance.

Smile an umbrella, a shield against drunks below. Sunset the cops
circled the house, lights whirling atop cars, blood drooling down
landlady's eyes, nose, mouth when they led her out.

Landlady's face the face of dead doe hung upside down in a shed.
Eyes corpse eyes. Told me once her father was Cherokee. Mumbled
Hated the fuckin' drunk made life hell.

Every other person in America a Cherokee. Must be something
in the polluted water. *Cherokee Nation,* hey, some of my best friends.

Every so often, in the middles of the nights, gunshots close by.
Bed pushed against front room wall so the cigarette smoke
won't cause an asthma attack. Can bullets pierce wall?

My brown tabby Persian cat trembling from the guns'
loud cracks. Crying tears into her soft fur and terrified body.

A nephew's wedding. Sister and oldest brother and me dancing
because we've drunk away our shyness. Dancing and laughing
to Chubby Checker's "The Twist" that way we used to.

Drinking. O *isn't it like the days of freedom when our people
stole horses and rode them without getting black and blue?
Without ever getting Blue? Before all the suicides?*

Brother leaping up into air as we did the twist. Flying,
soaring like an eagle. Twisting beneath American flag
in an American Legion Hall off a parkway of neon lights.

Laughing. We couldn't stop laughing.

Homeless on Bleeker Street

I.

After I read at the Bowery Poets' Club with other ugly poets
to celebrate *Ugly Poets, Beautiful Poems* anthology we all
have beautiful poems of rapes, name-callings, shame,
poverty-strickenness, cancers, deaths and indomitable
love in, I start tramping back through The Village to
Washington Square Hotel where I got a room with
500 dollars a rich professor promised me for editing
her latest manuscript ... boring poems I'd so far only
glanced at before returning to my own. My poet friends
snickered about the hotel thing, lay bets on whether
I'd finish the manuscript so I could pay for three day
splurge in this ugly-beautiful city of a million poets.
And that was "all good." I placed my own bet on
whether the winner would ever collect. What a poor lot ...
but *rich in spirit*, as any self-respecting poet might say.

II.

Growing poorer by the minute, I right angle off
Bowery onto Bleeker Street, hoping I don't get lost
in Greenwich Village, again. I almost trip over two sneakers
silhouetted in tatters against sidewalk. Black-and-white
gym shoes like those my brothers wore when they played
basketball back in 1960s, when everything carried the sheen
of innocence ... or at least gleaming pretense. When they
played in ankle-high shoes I was still a Catskill girl who had
never seen Manhattan, a "part Indian" who listened at night
to trucks on Route 17, dream-hitchhiking my way to the coast,
to ocean I yearned to see. Now these sneakers from the torn
past. Then the cardboard sign, black marker plea: *Please
help me. All my things were stolen from me in a shelter.
I need money for clothes, food. Thank you. I bless you.*

Hands that look frozen even in June. Young man's face,
hollow HIV cheeks. Eyes that must have been a cat's eyes
before their emerald turned sick.

III.

I have been trying my hardest to be New York-hard, not give
money to every musician, dancer, comedian, panhandler
I meet on the street or in subways. I'm not worth that much,
know *There but for the grace of God go I*, especially if I
keep giving away what little I have. Yet thinking of grace
and of how I am graced still, I kneel, give this young man
some crumpled dollars. I don't know why I do it, but I squat
next to him, ask how he ended up homeless on Bleeker Street.
I even ask him his name. "Todd," he says. I don't say
"Todd" means "death" in German, that death haunts
the thinness of his hands and eyes. So I sit cross-legged
among gum wads, spit, broken glass ... for over an hour
listen to Todd tell me about dead parents, smack addiction,
shelters where people guard their last belongings by sleeping
on them. How when anyone invites him to stay at their place
they always turn out to be crazy.

IV.

This is how I end up on Bleeker Street, after picking my way
over Thunderbird bottles winos shattered on Bowery pavement.
How I knelt on hot cement with Todd, watching men, women,
even children trying not to see us, praying the cops also
wouldn't notice us ... green-eyed young man in 60s' shoes ...
green-eyed Native poet with long white hair, hippie skirt,
Mohawk earrings, and a vision-hunt happening in her heart.
Todd, my brother, this heart has panhandled for the tossed
coins of recognition all my life ... begging those who didn't
grow up Indian or poor or in the mountains or wildly poetic
to take *one* look at what it's like before they scurry home
to their safe lives. Here on Bleeker Street I can glimpse

homeless ghosts of Manhattan's first people in this city
of Trumps where I, too, eventually hurry on to three days
of transient safety in Washington Square, blessing
jingling in my empty pockets.

A Winter Poem of Making Love

We walked at the edge of Lily Lake.
    Love new. Snow new
        and so high we stumbled as if drunk.

Then we saw the place where the deer slept.
    You slipped off your fern green coat.
        You lay it across the dreams of deer.

You covered me like new sky beneath the bowed pines.

Zen Board for a Beloved Warrior

You gave me a Zen board for my birthday,
white sky on which to brush words, images,
that would flee quickly as life. Each day
I left my heart's calligraphy on the board.
Sometimes you and I painted love strokes
for each other. Soon … sky, again.

Yes, you gave me a Zen board during a moon
of blaze. Each dawn I stumble to its sky,
write a morning prayer for you, not knowing
what might happen to you that day in jail. I take
my memory of the night the cops dragged you away …
not knowing anything for the first five days
you were caged … turn my grief into silent chant.

I wake thinking of that first time I drove to visit you
in an ice storm's high noon twilight, not caring if I slid
off highway and died except I needed to keep living
for you. I shiver to sleep hearing your phone call
after our visit, how they strip-searched you on your way
back to A-pod. *Made me take off the orange jump suit,
stand naked, raise my arms up, lift my balls, squat, cough.*

Each night I crash into nightmares, thinking
of you on mattress thin as a poor man's justice.
My very bones hear your soundless weeping
and dream of bringing your bare brush strokes
home to the Zen board of our bed, my love.

11 at Night, Fall

Somewhere between early morning
and 11 at night, you realize
you will never love anyone again.

Not in that way.

You don't know why you know this.

Maybe because this day is halfway
between autumn equinox and summer solstice.

You have washed the Cold Mountain of dishes.

You have typed the secret caves of your last poem.

Your Persian cat, Wu Wei, is doing nothing
in brown tabby sleep across claw-torn chair.

On chipped wall a blue poster, Woody Guthrie …
I hate a song that makes you think you are not any good.

1948 Billie Holiday poster next to Woody. Also blue.

Beatific smile on her beat up face, too.

Wu Wei

Named her Wu Wei
because she was a brown tabby
Persian cat with pointy white beard
and Mongolian eyes

who appeared like
an ancient Chinese poet
staring from pet store cage,
Doing Nothing …

and since I could not bear
the thought of any poet
desolate behind bars
I bought her for Christmas,

gift for me and younger
Korean lover, yes, a poet
I took up with after I left
the husband who caged me.

Wu Wei, my lover, and I …
a trilogy of poetry sprung
from sadness into tenderness,
our love eternal

as the old bards sang.
Poetry man married now,
has a little daughter.
Mid-summer I had to have

Wu Wei "put to sleep,"
during a tornado warning
drove her to where my poet and I
once made love in winter woods

atop his coat spread on snow
where deer slept near lake,
where I left bones and fur
silken like my poet's hair.

Two Indian Visions

I.

They don't send smoke signals from
horizons anymore. Instead, they chat
on cell phones using unlimited Verizons.
Being Indian, sooner or later they mention
Mother Earth, woman confiding to man
she drives deep into the Catskills
when she needs to heal, bring
her spirit back into balance.

Like that autumn, she says, *when I was still
with that white man and he yanked my long hair,
nearly broke my neck. I went to where my great uncle
lived in solitude after his divorce. I walked
in a sacred circle around the lake, lay on
dirt, leaves, until a voice breathed "Everything
will be okay."* Same words my father breathed
before his last breath. Woman adds, *When I cry
for a vision it comes as quiet wind, it comes as light.*

II.

I know what you mean, the man's voice swoops
sweetly, hotly, across the free miles.
I always go back to nature for my visions, too.
Yeah, right, she thinks, *this Métis
who fought his way up on city streets,
just went to a wake for a Mick mobster.*
Not that he wasn't a poet, too, not that
he wasn't Indian, too, except he was of Hurons
who named her people Mohawks, *Man-Eaters.*

I know you're going to say something
smart-mouthed, she warns, wondering how
his raw heart would taste with meat tenderizer on it.
No, noooo, he lilts too sweetly. *I had a similar*
experience in Nova Scotia years ago when I
wandered out on the peninsula during a bad time
in my life. I gazed at Father Sun fancy dancing
on the Big Water and called for an answer.
At last I heard a Voice say, "I'm sorry,
the party you are calling isn't answering."

Crossing Over Mid-Hudson Bridge After Sunset

By the time I get on the Bridge I feel kind of crazy ... not sure
I took the right exit to get there. I drove an elder poet around
a traffic circle once ... "Slow down," she cried, "slow down!
This makes me feel as if we're going to fly right up in the air.
Only a man could think something like this up!" And *that* is
how I felt, jerking steering wheel so old Indian car could zip
into narrow road twisting up to Mid-Hudson Bridge. Now here
it seems worth the skipped heart beats, that *I might fly off
the road* feeling, my fear of flying. Now I *am* flying between
suspension bridge arches, locked in single file car flow, taillights
ruby ahead ... eyes half-hallucinating from jewels of headlights
rushing, flashing at me in opposite lane, white, white, white
circles of pearls in the oyster of night. Arches rise high, swoop
down, then up again, supported by long silver verticals of
steel. It is all so *pretty* ... a child's word for it, but that is what
soars with me as I glide over deep, indigo river below ...
smiling insanely at little lights that perch along arches, tiny birds
of purple, green, blue, red. Every so often I glance northward
towards Hudson, twinklings of shore lights fancy dancing on water,
Mother Earth embracing river from mirroring sides. And in
Sky World a trace of sunset, faint trail of Cherokee red.
I think of the Trail of Tears, of trails that brought me here.
I think about how polluted the Hudson is, about the deformed
fish, how no Indian in her right mind would eat anything
out of this river that steals my heart whenever I see it,
makes me fall in love for the first time no matter how often
I behold it, despite toxins from cars, trucks, motorcycles,
factories blotting the dark banks. I know what it means
to not know the ancient language that would give me
the Native name for *Hudson* that shape-shifts into Eagle
inside whatever in me is broken ... fills me with wings
by the time I reach the Bridge's opposite end. Lights flash
more than ever in my eyes, fractals of tears, and I turn up
air-conditioner and Tom Waits' "The Ghosts of Saturday Night,"

roaring off Mid-Hudson Bridge, love flamed out of centuries
of heartbreak soaring with me, weeping from the beauty
of this night, this river, this Bridge, O this *mystery* electric-lit.

I Am Taking the A-Train

Snow frosting third floor windows, me back in one city
but holding onto love in another ... to Valentine's Eve
riding Greyhound from Binghamton to meet you
in Washington Heights' apartment. For the first time
I braved New York's subway alone, half-ran through
Port Authority past Peruvian musicians who always
seem to play there, down to tracks, tunnels, gangsta rats
scurrying between gleaming rails. Asking New Yorkers
of every color, *blood*, language, which train to take, grinning
when they said, "Take the A Train," because I jumped
on that train four decades ago, bought 78 LP with The Duke
playing IT, trumpet seducing me into leaving girlhood Catskills
for skyscraper peaks. Man, I really believed skyscrapers
kissed the sky until a cousin drove me to The City and I
realized not even the Empire State Building swayed that high.
But I could still hear the soar of Duke's "Take the A-Train"
on virgin tour of neon city my Indian heart yearned
to be a beatific poet in despite Bowery winos wiping
car windows with delirium tremors rags and strung out
hookers crooking fishnet legs at us. Or did I hear that music
because of those gutter angels? Yeah, I grinned wide
when the nicest city slickers in the galaxy guided me
to the A-Train so I might ride it up Manhattan's hard, long,
funky, sleepless body to where you would meet me that night,
and I laughing, remembering cousin's warning, "Don't speak
to New Yorkers, bunch of Mac the Knifes." Who knows
why no Macs mugged me Valentine's night? Did they pay
homage to my face tattooed with 18th anniversary of mother's
breast cancer death? Smell them ole NDN blues on me
even when headed for the Heights to meet you, eagle-eyed
man who calls me "soul mate" and his "sacred space" and
all those crazy corny sincere words lovers bless the empty
places with? Maybe urban renegades spotted the dance
of ghost kisses on my lips, cheeks, ears, grooved on how

it was going to feel so good to me, so grand to me, once I
stepped into the A-Train's lit-up hollow, rocking in timeless
express rush through underground darknesses, flashings,
keeping my face to myself the way women do on A-Train
dreaming its way to hilly, hopeful sprawl of bodegas,
street hustles, Hudson River breezes and hip hop visions
where taxi drivers refuse to go. But I flew there, free
as a trumpet gone wild, gold cat flecks in eyes jamming
with A-Train lights, because no one dare mug
some Mohawk so fired with hot jazz of riding
underground towards night of rapture in orange haze
by tall window opening out to undulations of Heights,
twinklings of a million apartments, windows, mad
musics and madder lovemakings. No one dare
touch that *crazy* except you so Valentine-hot,
so Ellington-cool. Yeah, I'm derailed back in
Binghamton and winter is a blizzard, but Baby,
I'm still taking that A-Train.

Part III

Carlos

My little brother, Carlos, would not open
his eyes. Three years eyes stayed shut.
Village doctor said, "Nothing wrong
with this boy's eyes. Nada." We cried,
"Carlos, you gotta open your eyes back up."

Amherst, Massachusetts. Listening
to Mayan woman while awaiting
Manhattan poet friend to ride in on
November night bus. Immigrant woman
like a fallen leaf in Indian summer night.

You often joke with New Englanders,
I'm the Indian responsible for your endless
Indian Summer. But nothing is funny
about this woman who grabs your arm,
speaks of working with Rigoberta Menchu

for Mayan rights. Her voice beer-soaked …
accented word slurs … you share stories
of invaders murdering your tribes. I sigh
My friend and I are going to a poets' conference
on genocide. Guess what? No Natives reading.

On this November night … *Carlos was three*
when he closed his sparkling eyes. I know why
he wouldn't open them. He seen too much.
Carlos don't wish to see more. Mi poor hermano.
New friend shuts *her* eyes. Tears tremble

down lashes. Like laughing leaves, others gust by
in town named for general who ordered soldiers
to give smallpox-infected blankets to freezing Indians.

Oh, these pale invaders possess hearts after all.
Invisible in black sky … Canadian geese cries.

Visible in red heart … *Indigenous sister's face*
like deep earth torn from Guatemala,
stolen land in displaced flesh, rainforest
tears muddying cheeks, lips. Two Indians
weeping on street paved in gold

light and ghosts, Mayan eyes like Carlos'
closed, Mohawk eyes no longer able to shut.

Ice Storm

In the middle of the night she heard it ...
low chiming outside, earth music
like crystal wine glasses falling,
delicate shatterings waving empty
across crusted snow.

Maybe she was dreaming
the bell-like breakings, except
sliver of sky shimmered
in the drunk dark, so she thought
her eyes must be open,

she must be awake
beneath fern-green quilt
a mountain grandmother made
decades ago, "geese flying south"
over naked skin,

her nakedness
and that strange ice music
glimmering
like last love, while

on Earth's other side
bombs were falling
on sand and desert city.
A woman lay there, also, listening
to glass shattering, thinking
Maybe I'm dreaming. Praying

she and her babies
breaking
into a thousand pieces
were not really awake,

weeping for her nakedness
to feel her man again
as geese flying south …

In the middle of the night she heard it.

Bluebird

She expected nothing. Was it an Indian thing?
Or just human, too many years of wintercounts
that after awhile can feel like dying? She

driving old Indian car, Purple Wampum Pony,
grey with dirt, wandering back roads to nowhere
on February anniversary of her mother's death,

yet even so feeling sun warming her face, ancient
panther body stretching out gold, soft, hot
in light, blood yearnings defying extinction,

when there appeared fancy dancing on birch
a bluebird, pale breast singed with sunrise
orange, wings lifting azure to blue sky. And

how would this college educated Indian explain
the bluebird of happiness danced "hello" to her
without making some post modern joke about it?

Still, the far back Indian in her, an old buried
sweetness, knew the bluebird was Mother,
blue fire flying into morning winterscape

before predicted blizzard began icing in,
she sliding into wildness bluer than grace,
wing flash of happiness.

When It Snows Women
Hold Quieter Times in Their Hands

Ice gardenias swirl from sky dark as Lady Day's hair,
no sound. Snow petals touch to earth, touch
after touch, and isn't it all so soft
as kiss after kiss?

And nowhere to go, roads un-ploughed.

We talk of this afterwards ...
what we women did that day similar to long slow days
of our grandmothers and great grandmothers.

One of us baked bread for the other women in her house.

One of us strung a necklace of glass beads color of her sister's eyes.

One of us wrote a letter the old way, in green calligraphy, for her man.

One of us dreamed a poem by west window while her cat chased snow.

I was the one who tugged on white buffalo coat and sheepskin boots,
trudged through storm to forge a snow angel with the wings of my arms
flying in the rapture of millions of snow crystals making unique
love to my mouth, cheeks, eyelids, hair.

We women speak of that Catskill snowfall even now ...
as my grandmother used to tell me of the days of sleighs and horses
and flashing bells, and once inside the house the kerosene lamps lit,
hands held near woodstove flames before her father took his fiddle out.

When it snows we women say *we wish, we wish,*
yearn for the prancing horses, bells, the fiddler's music,
ancient dance so wild and whirling ...

when women hold quieter times in their hands.

Martin Luther King, Jr. Night

Especially silent night on city South Side
Could be any northern city in any anonymous dark

Unless they must trudge out
City dwellers burrowed far inside walls

Weather calls for snow and ice
Breeze jangles glass wind chimes

Behind lace curtains blinds shut
On lap Persian cat she and Korean lover got

Purrs   slant of half-closed eyes
Glow of Silk Road Dreamtime

Remembering tales of women who lost
Their one true love

Wandering by midnight seas
Turning to stone and gorse on cliffs and heaths

Despite trailing skirt   tangled hair
She doesn't ramble except in heather heart

No train whistle keens up from river valley
Invisibly its old city shimmers   lost galaxy

Along ice-jammed river
Snow shrouded earth   buried memories

She and lover winging snow angels
Beneath violet sky   astral snowfall

She thinks of storm approaching
Outside the blinds   of outsiders like her

And January-born King   skin deep night
Voice   whirlwind of crystals

Dream   blaze on hope's mountaintop
All Earth's snow angels rising up

Playing Marbles

They were talking over the phone about February,
the way winter drags on, how they used to play marbles
at the first sign of thaw. They marveled at why kids
no longer play marbles. The younger sister said
sometimes she discovered lost marbles or shards
of them gleaming in dirt by the old schoolhouse.
She always carried such treasures home
to place around flower pots. They spoke
about crystals, aggies, cat's eyes, their colors
far prettier than jewels. The elder sister asked,
"Do you still have our marbles? When I visit
the Catskills, let's shoot marbles in the melting
snow." They both started laughing. *What?*
Them lose their marbles? They mourned
those who had metamorphosed to zombies,
the "grown ups" who believed it foolish
to pump themselves up on swings to see
if they might touch the sky. Come spring,
they vowed once more they'd swing high, fly
over sparkles beading Willowemoc River,
hair lifting in sun as silver wings. They
agreed to keep childlikeness in their hearts.
Nor did they use any big words like *God*.
They didn't need to. Rolling the sacred hoops
of marbles across snow crystals, dreaming
towards the light until they were eagles,
was enough.

Baloney

After months of chilling nor'easters, this endless winter
the doomsayers gloat is the greenhouse effect ...
flu weakening you the way invaders' viruses once ravaged
ancestors, Mohawk and Blackfoot ... you decide to venture
back out into the frightened world. "The human body
can't take the erratic weather," a friend consoled you.
"We simply break down." Outside, late March sun
glitters off your body as it glitters off cracked
ice on the pond. Inside your bones' snow-lit darkness
nor'easters still howl across tundras of frozen pain.
Too weak to fix lunch, you drive to the nearest plaza,
another ghost mall, a few stores left. SUBWAY sign jumps
your eyes in browns, whites, yellows. The ugly power
of its advertising carves in you a craving for a big, fat, phallic
sub. You enter this fast food place that only America
could think up, briefly dreaming you're strong enough
to re-enter what passes for the land-of-the-living.

There's something about the smell of dead meat
coupled with hot peppers, pickles and Sicilian olives.
"Can I help you?" a curly haired man in a SUBWAY version
of Stanley Kowalski's tee shirt leers. "I'll have the twelve inch
Classic Italian," you drawl. "Pepperoni, salami, ham and ...
baloney," you pronounce the SUBWAY listing bologna,
as though spelling it so could make baloney other than
what it is. "And what fixings do you want?" The man fingers
a manager's patch on his stained shirt. "I want it all,"
you make love with your eyes to the side-by-side steel bins
of tempting condiments. "But I don't want any baloney.
Could you please leave out the baloney and lay on some extra
Genoa salami?" "I can't do that," the manager projects
his paunch across the pickles. "We can only take things
away. We can't add."

You study your hands spread against the garish yellow counter,
remembering the 1950s and 1960s, growing up in Catskills,
year after year of being served baloney on Wonder Bread,
year after year of baloney slithering off the white bread
of teachers' tongues, year after year of being poor and keeping
silent. "I don't get it," you half laugh. "I don't see why
I can't skip your baloney and have more salami." Inside
the laughter you're beginning to feel flu-weak again, wishing
you were inside your sickbed inside four safe walls too sick
to care about this living. And you're trying not to take
any of it personally, trying not to believe this "baloney thing"
has anything to do with your black coat flowing to floor,
or beaded earrings glinting lavender off your ears,
or silvery hair shooting out static electricity. Does he
suspect you're Indian? Has he guessed you've gone hungry
and been poor? Does your soft voice smoke-signal
he can push you around? So you insist, "WHY?"

"Because those are my orders," he boasts. "Everything is
prearranged. Of course, being the manager, I can insert more
salami into your roll … if you're willing to pay four dollars
for it." "BA-LO-NEY," you shrug, turning your black back
on him, biting into your tongue the words you'd like to scream,
"I wouldn't pay four cents for your salami, given that you're
another ball-less excuse of a 21st century man just following
orders. I thank the Cosmos and Poetic Chaos that I'm beyond
all help in your ordered world." But he probably has a family
to support and can't risk losing his job, so you dawdle

in your old silence out the door into sunlight, down
the sidewalk to China Wok. You order Chinese food
from a young Chinese woman whose cheekbones and eyes
glowing beneath epicanthic eyelids cause you to wonder
if your ancestors ever crossed paths on the Bering Strait.
No baloney here. When she gives you your food, you wish
each other "good day," the food inside its paper bag steaming
up like summer into your face, voices together a fragrant song.

At home, first thing you do is crack open a fortune cookie.
Its tiny slip of paper reads, "Your wisdom will find a way."
You uncover the food you chose, celestial couplings
of miniature corn, snow peas, broccoli, strange mushrooms,
succulent vegetables you have no names for. You bask
in sunlight streaming through the bay window, snow melting
off trees. Sometimes when you refuse to accept baloney
you end up with Buddha's Feast.

Skating

Even though it had been years since she skated,
hair lightened to that ice she once glided over ...
skating on winter nights beneath snow crystal stars
became her recurring dream. This evening
spring snow like vast swan wings enfolded
muddy Earth, the old dream shimmering in
with storm, she a green-eyed Indian girl again,
"mixed-blood" limbs twirling and leaping
across the pond. And green-eyed Indian man
she laughed with under a great tree
in March Saturday's morning hours ...
tree-tall himself ... shape-shifts back to
half-breed boy skating free in her dream.

Beautiful boy ... snow skin not yet lashed
by hockey scars, from colonized father and
world's hardness and recurring nightmare
of disease. In this return under eyelids, dream boy
and dreaming girl shining like birds in sheltering tree,
grabbing each other's hands, skating faster, flying,
skate blades silver flames and high boned cheeks
fire in freezing wind, Indian children rising off
ice with no memories of pain, cracking
the whip of each other against the black
world like an unseen noose tightening
around the pond.

Red Lake

Waking to dawn rain on windowpane,
storm greening earth after hard winter.
Easter Monday … snuggled with cat
beneath quilts, tired but blissful
from family celebration of great niece
entering springtime world. Skin grown
quiet with rain light and cat purrs. Falling
rain-like back to sleep, waking later
to stumble down stairs.

Over coffee reading yesterday's news.
Boy at Red Lake Reservation … shot others,
then himself. Now everybody making time
to analyze the dead Indian boy's rage.
Look around. Hasn't Mother Earth
shape-shifted into one big rez?
Lakes of blood everywhere?

Remembering cradling great niece,
tiny traveler at two months. Stop
walking with her, she weeps.
Drifting back to girlhood daydreams
of hopping boats, trains, planes
to different lands. Is this unrest
in your people's blood? A distrust
we are born with … tumbling
into this Turtle Island of ghosts,
then running elsewhere?

Great niece, hair tinted sunrise red …
Red Lake boy, Raven's hair twisted
into black horns, self-dubbed *NativeNazi*,

alien to the beautiful old names that rose
from dream or vision or elders' long observance.
What might have saved the Chippewa boy from hate?

Maybe such heart as yours this Easter Monday …
listening to rain, breathing in flowering air,
mingling silver hair with Persian's gold fur.
And smiling at rain drops jingle-dancing across
windows, you curled cat-like in rocking chair where
parents sang to you when you were as great niece,
drifting back to when the People took the time.

It's Easy When You Love an Indian in Prison

It's not that I don't feel bad about Leonard Peltier. I remember
those AIM days, how my heart vibrated to the drums
and my tongue longed to honor our warriors with its tremolo
mute for so long. I believed the American Indian Movement
would give us our pride back. And as far as I can tell,
Leonard was given a bad rap. Yeah, I phoned Bill Clinton
before he left office. I told the woman who answered
I thought President Clinton with his drop of Cherokee blood
should grant a pardon to Leonard Peltier. She said,
"Who's Leonard Peltier?" Leonard didn't get his pardon.
He still gets to be America's numero uno political prisoner.

It's easy when you love an Indian in prison. You can
splash his face on your MySpace, Facebook, Blog, website,
stick FREE LEONARD PELTIER bumpersticker on SUV
rear end, even send checks for his legal defense team.
If you are a poet, you get to write your Leonard Peltier poem.
As you may have noticed, this is mine. It's a breeze when you love
an Indian in solitary in the belly of the bloated beast. This Indian
thanks you for caring. Nya'weh. But if Leonard is released
will you treat him the way you treat me and others who don't
thrill you the way an Indian accused of murdering an FBI Agent
gives you wet dreams? We who are not "noble savage" enough?

Because ... I don't remember you inviting me to dine
at your house. When did you ever ask me to sleep in one
of your beds, rest a few days away from my desperate life?
I don't have honoring stories to tell about the times I cried
and you caught my tears in hands like holy grails.
I do have stories about words you massacred me with
when no one "important" was around, "Sorry, you don't
look Indian. You've got green eyes and light skin." Hell,
you and your smile don't look racist or rude. Here's medicine
one AIM bro' gave me once: "They mention your *white blood*

to control you. Tell those colonial motherfuckers it's *your* land. They don't get to talk about you because they're not Indian. They can shut up and doggy paddle back to their so-called old country."

Isn't it easy when you love an Indian in prison?

The Anti-Bukowski

Had I a dollar for each time a young male writer
bragged his favorite poet is Charles Bukowski
I'd bag a poetry stipend for life, use it for
moving to the green woods and never again
risk a close encounter of the vomiting kind
with a Bukowski wannabe thinking

drinking, drugging, cursing, and treating
women like fast food equates being a bard.
Once I met a guy named Dan who worked
at Starbucks to survive. When Dan heard
I was a poor, disgraced, ostracized poet
he told me his old man and Charles Bukowski

hung out in the same Long Beach dive. Dan
was still a boy but his father dragged him along
because, hell, there was no place else to ditch him.
"Bukowski was obnoxious when he drank,"
Dan confided over the coffee machines' grind,
"a total pig to the ladies. One afternoon

I couldn't take his big mouth anymore.
'Bukowski,' I yelled, 'all you are is a limp
prick, a mean drunk who hates women,
and a crappy poet who impresses no one
except other alchie assholes like yourself.'"
Dan shook his head. "I was certain Chuck

was gonna deck me when he lunged across
the floor, me ducking to miss his ham
of a hand. But instead of a fist he formed
a fan with his fingers, fluttering them through
my hair. 'You know what, kid,' he growled,
'you're all right,' then prowled back

to where a redhead swiveled on a bar stool,
lip synching to jukebox love songs, not seeing
she was about to be Chuck's next laid McMuffin."
Bukowski, clown briefly clear enough to praise
a boy who smashed his glass of B.S. ...
Bukowski wannabes, assholes who can't write.

One Night, Two Poets

discovered the countries of themselves
sharing wine in what appeared to be a garret.
"How did we get here?" they howled
between kisses, twenty stories high
in an American city. A panther stared
out the window, remembering itself
before it became extinct. In Sky World
Grandmother Moon spun around as if
men had torn into her again, knocked
fullness off balance.

The poets drank naked.

The woman poet smiled, "Baudelaire wrote poems
while balling his black mistress in their Paris garret.
I've longed to try that with an Indian man."
Paper possibilities flared through the window, pens
flowered like eagle feathers inside their hands. The man
let the wine bottle glisten to floor. The woman flung
clay cup at ceiling, wine laughing as Aurora Borealis
across winter paint. She spread her legs like wings
in a parallel universe. He grew a second body of light,
scattering stars inside her flying. Stars blossomed
into constellation. Nine months later
they gave their poem a name.

Long Dirt Nap

People speak of Heaven, Paradise, the Spirit World.
I know I once read something about good Muslim men
rewarded with virgins in a verdant garden
after they depart here. Mostly, no one wants to die
and have done with it. They plan to have it all
afterlife-nice, even though niceness bores them
in their earthly life. I don't notice people plucking
gold harps while sprouting angel wings on the street
where I live. Those with some divine Hallucination
on their side would burn me as a witch if they could.
I don't know who abandoned me in this movie,
who assigned me this star role of Indian poet,
an actress with love medicine who even so
doesn't care if she has a man. I don't understand
why the ones bent on ascending to Pearly Gates, etc.,
hate me so much. *What did I do!?* Don't expect me
to apologize if you are seeing multiple orgasms
inscribed in the light of my face. Don't expect me
to beg when you go to kick me because my eyes
glow with stories in a way that your dull jealousies
never will. Don't count on me to stop smiling forever
when you stab me with such cruel words that I
become Blanche DuBois lamenting with tear-stained
tongue, "Deliberate cruelty is not forgivable.
It's one thing I've never been guilty of." I don't
ask for much. I am satisfied with being bedazzling
for a brief sojourn on a blue planet in a minority galaxy.
I'll take writing an occasional poem like an ultimate
kiss. I'll take a friend spontaneously singing
an old ballad to me. I'll embrace my cat, Wu Wei,
Doing Nothing purring near my body that is nothing
but a shooting star, considered lucky but soon gone.

Those God-spouters can have their afterlife. I hold
with what an Indian bro' calls it … a long dirt nap.
For my paradise, I would be wild mountain laurel
growing from my dreamer's heart.

This Jesus Cat

This Jesus cat landed on the short list for a Poet's position
at a major university. Day before he wandered in to be
interviewed and meet all the appropriate professors,

a theorist outside the Creative Writing Program
noticed that this Jesus cat's dossier lacked transcripts
from any colleges, major or minor. Whispers

whizzed through English Department hallways
like knives flying at an infant's back. I bet this Jesus cat
knows someone high up ... Yeah, who did he sleep with?

Whose feet did he wash that got his hand washed
in turn? Being civilized and civil, the professors
maintained their Anglophiliac smiles the following day

when this Jesus cat in sandals, long hair and red poncho
flowed into the Chair's office as if fancy dancing on water,
flashed the peace sign at where she sat in uptight suit.

The professors had to admire this Jesus cat's glowing
fingers, ones responsible for those exquisite parable poems
and eloquent narrative pieces included in his application,

although some had bemoaned his sending poetry
on a scroll of wine-stained parchment. Others noticed
he had the hands of a carpenter or someone of that ilk,

much like the scarred hands of their fathers whose jobs
they didn't speak about. So the English Department's
wannabe aristocrats interviewed this Jesus cat while

plotting how they were going to explain in tongues coated
with aspartame that they could never hire a brilliant poet
sans even a B.A., it was de rigueur in a college of the crème

de la crème to hire MFA Program poets, even if age ten.
Besides that, the professors had to admit this Jesus cat
aroused long forgotten fancies in evocative ways, including

his reference letters from Hiawatha, Crazy Horse and
Geronimo. But après the initial frisson of those, even
the letters made them cringe. What if Homeland Security

got on the Department's case? A few renegade professors
who hadn't utterly learned to garble bolder utterances
in Derrida-speak, enthused that this Jesus cat

might make a really great teacher. In his letter
to the Search Committee he had made it midnight clear
he was a peacenik and long time advocate

for women's equality, the poor, the homeless, and people
of color and colorfulness. Yes, there were those who were
truly moved by this Jesus cat's soaring descriptions of

roaming homeless himself across the land and sleeping out
by fires under ancient stars and living like those Indians
who had given him Confidential Letters of Reference.

The Committee suspected this poet might be Indian, too,
and if he had a CDIB card he could make things look
God Almighty good vis-à-vis the English Department's

gaining more diversity after years of hiring the white,
the already comfortable, the secretly racist, and no Indians.
Yea, this Jesus cat they already knew they were gonna crucify.

Rides High Horses

I forgot to tell you my dream, the winter's night
I cried for your lost long hair ... stumbled
through forest gathering its soft feathers
of starlit blackness. I forgot this dream

in between our phone talk and laughter, yes,
in between our happy *bullshit,* as you call it,

how I cradled the broken-winged ravens
of your sun-bringing hair in my hands,
desperate to return the strands to you ...

the prayer hair of Shawnees, the raped
stolen land, your warrior's life choked
by words like *lawyers, mortgages, banks.*

I forgot to tell you because we kept
swapping stories of bravery. I bragged
I leapt on my high horse when the landlord
tried to raise my rent again, you laughing

at five feet two me and my tomahawk
until I tittered, "Oh, so you know
about riding on a high horse?"

"I have a whole herd of high horses," you boasted,

voice gleaming with southern Illinois breezes
and slow streams of your first language, some
gentleness invaders could not cut from your tongue.

Maybe this will be my Indian name for you ...
Rides High Horses. Aho.

The Gingrich Who Stole Christmas

Behold the Christ Child born again in a barn outside
Bethlehem, PA! Mary, in her long blue dress, bundles
Jesus in a coat from Catholic Charities. His tiny fingers reach
for her dark tresses, his brown eyes flash with light from the star
of Bethlehem flooding the open door. Joseph kneels, wraps them
both inside his warming arms. Beyond the barn snow sparkles
in long drifts to the town's star-crowned Christmas trees. Faraway
voices, little bells, chime in wonder, "What child is this?"
The organic farmers, who sheltered Joseph and Mary here,
kneel among the lowing cows. God's angel still sings
in the farmers' ears, "Joy, Joy, good tidings of great Joy,"
great wings beating inside their burgeoning hearts.

Behold the Christ Child crying. *What is happening, Mommy?*
See them, three social workers bearing official documents.
Where are the three Wise Men bearing treasures of gold,
frankincense and myrrh? Hear them: "The Gingrich, Speaker
of the House, has decreed this child be placed in an orphanage.
The boy was conceived by an unwed teenaged mother ...
a mixed-blood babe since this Jewish girl insists the babe's father
is God. She is wanton, having convinced that bearded hippie, Joseph,
to protect her. We will have no more of the poor having babies,
or immoral counterculture families with two fathers, and absolutely
no infants being raised by misfits who hear angels telling them
their offspring are the children of God."

"The Gingrich himself would note it's midnight-clear
that up to 25% of the riffraff and lowing cows in this barn
did illegal drugs in the past five years. How else account
for all those angels and holy ghosts? Once we shoot up
Joseph and Mary with thorazine, we'll eliminate these
hallucinations. As for their infant, Jesus, it's the orphanage
for him. If he's lucky, some well-off family will adopt him,
twist him into a proper Christian product like The Gingrich.

He'll despise the poor, cut off the hapless and hungry
from welfare, Medicaid, food stamps, channel the leftover
dough to the truly deserving, the tax-starved rich. And
should this Jesus take after his parents, thinking he hears
the voice of God, or believing he is God, we'll nail him
to the cross of psychotropic drugs."

Behold the Christ Child born again in a barn outside
Bethlehem, PA. *Mommy, don't let them take me.*
I came back to tell them they got it wrong for two millennia.
Didn't I say blessed are the poor for theirs is the kingdom
of God? Didn't I say blessed are they that weep now for they
shall laugh? Didn't I come to heal the broken-hearted?
What did I tell them about little children, and about praying
in private instead of loudly, like hypocrites, in public?
And when did I ever command the slaughter of millions
of Jews, Moslems, Indians, Africans ... who haven't they
murdered in my name? As for women, I loved women
and they loved me. Mary Magdalene was my dearly beloved,
closest of all disciples. How could they burn as witches
the women who burned with vision? In my Father's House
are many mansions, but does The Gingrich, Speaker
of the House, dwell there?

All across America Christmas lights are blowing out,
star-crowned trees dying beneath cheap tinsel. All across
America the children of God are crying for wise men
to bring them treasures, the gold of tenderness, frankincense
of kindness, myrrh of joy. The snow's sparkle fades
with dawn's incoming storm. Levitating off billboards,
Joe Camel passes smugly through the needle's eye.
The trucks of commerce pass on the highway, the cows
must be milked. Joseph and Mary no longer hear the voices
of angels, only the voices of politicians. "Jesus, these poor
are hopeless. Christ, we can't tolerate it anymore."

Behold the Christ Child unable to speak like The Gingrich.
Ecce the Child, light born as flesh, born again in a barn
outside Bethlehem. See the shining-eyed child of the poor
pulled from his mother's arms and Joseph's arms trying
to blanket them both … God made so human he can
only weep.

Part IV

Part II

Ritual for My Father

1:30 a.m. October first, thirty third
anniversary of your death. Earlier tonight
I gazed long at a picture of you ...
so long it felt not even like time anymore.
Maybe it can be if one stares intensely enough
into an old photograph, a distant face,
the numbers will stop, eternity drop
by for a visit. I would make such a visitor
Eight O' Clock coffee as you once did
in aluminum drip pot that softened
our faces to silver rain. And

it did rain last day of September,
hours so depressed by clouds
it felt like winter solstice. But
no Christmas tree, fireplace fire
or bayberry candles to dispel
the damp dark. Main light
was you bordered by glass frame
hue of a Purple Heart. You ...
boy in ragged sweater raising
baby sister up towards sky.

O laughter of your upturned face,
smile before you joined the Marines,
were shot on Guam. Smile I never
got to see, smile you dreamed for me.
"Smile," you'd tease. "You are more
beautiful when you smile." Often
I have imagined knowing that 1940 boy
with epicanthic eyelids and green eyes
nearly disappearing when all his face opened
with joy. But I found you, scarred,

somehow more beautiful than the boy
raising the girl gazing intensely into
his face, short hungry fingers clutching
his knit hat as if begging, "Please stay here."
Later this morning I'll drink Eight O'Clock coffee.
After the hour of your death, in the dawn world
of betrayal and lies, I'll have my ritual of liquid
bitterness. Perhaps in your old drip pot
grief's rain will silver to smiles. Father,
maybe I'll be beautiful awhile.

Boots

Sometimes I can't keep silent anymore,
like tonight when a few Facebook friends
posted one of those pictures knee-jerking us
to "support our troops and honor the dead" ...

empty beaten boots in single file
lining tarmac in some flat treeless place,
each boot with dinky American flag poked in it
and 4x6 glossy of the deceased pinned to top,

underneath a cliché about the "heroes"
now theoretically bootless and happy in Heaven ...
how they "fought for our freedom." I hope so.
I hope I am mis-seeing because I don't see

as much freedom anymore. Yesterday
a university student told me his generation
feels afraid to speak up or take to the streets.
I asked "Why do you think that is?"

The sensitive young poet mentioned *"that law*
the Government passed" ... added "protesting
can get us arrested as terrorists." Where I survive
in an old upstate New York factory town

veterans who served time in Iraq and Afghanistan
were a part of the back door draft, poor, struggling,
in a city of shut downs and diminishing work ...
just hurt-eyed kids who thought being soldiers

would give them a shot at something better in life,
not get them shot. *"DEAD IS DEAD IS DEAD"*
I banged below the boots, flags and nothing words,
missing my dead father shot in "the Good War."

Is it freedom or the smug "one percent" and new
Gilded Age our children are getting faces blown off for?
And now the other back door draft ... student loans
turning poorer students into slaves for life.

Dead soldiers' boots on Facebook, what a kick.
How about a blow-up of the flag-draped coffins
we're kept from seeing ... pried wide open?
Then we can *Share* the remains of our freedom.

Dow Chemical

When we had our first fight over the war, I said
How would you like it if your son got sent there?

Your voice pierced polluted air with its usual Fox News tone.
I'd have no problem if my son bombed those Arab bastards

back to the Stone Age. I trembled *You know he won't go, even*
with a draft. A doctoral student at a top college? No way.

Their choice, you shot back. *No one forced those soldiers*
to enlist. I quavered rage then. *There's a back door draft.*

I've had students who joined because they couldn't afford
school. No money. No rich families to help out. No options.

It's a free country, you hissed. I asked *How would you like it*
if your son died in the desert or came home with his face half

gone, or his soul? Ever the smug Tea Partier, you oozed
I'd be proud if he died for freedom, as if the war wasn't

about black ooze of oil and the rich using quivering flesh
to stuff their greed more. Tonight my sister calls. Tells me

your son almost got blown up in some secret experiment
he and a friend were doing for Dow Chemical. Son

I pleaded with last Christmas, *I think it would be better*
if you became a professor. He had just strolled out the lab door,

who knows why. Friend still in the room when it exploded,
chemicals, metal, glass invading the country of his perfect body.

You and my brother hopped a plane South soon as you could.
Something about your boy being close to a nervous breakdown.

Sweet nephew I once cradled in my arms. I remember being
his age. The way I sought truth. Attended teach-ins. Tried

to find out if my country was raping another country ...
Vietnam. Learned Dow Chemical made napalm and Dial soap.

After, washing with Dial and ignorance seared my flesh. I stopped
such cleansing. After Dow Chemical nearly killed your son, will you?

Pollution

During phone calls we speak of days
we shared in Catskills before decades
of barely seeing each other ...
you in Maine, me everywhere.
Mostly I encounter your face
as dreamlike bas relief against
weddings and funerals
or rare holiday gatherings.

I suspect I must almost be a ghost to you.
Yet our voices recognize each other
from my girlhood entwined with your boyhood.

Today I phone because I am ill
from a flu shot and heard you were, too ...
both sick, secretly lost and afraid.

But raised to "keep going,"
we don't dwell on our fevers ...
wonder briefly if treated meats,
toxic air and poisoned waters
are making so many people sick.

I remind you of the June you read
Rachel Carson's *Silent Spring*,
when you helped me comprehend
why we no longer could swim
in Willowemoc swimming hole
beneath mountain bank white with laurel.

You helped our family understand
that word Dad brought home one evening
in his black lunch bucket ... *pollution*.
I can't even recall sound around

the supper table once he said
we no longer could go to the river.

You, my brother ...
our scientist, our caring boy,
who explained where the poisons came from,
why the birds stopped singing.

This morning you tell me a story
about the professor who asked
if you had plagiarized your paper
on pollution, doubting a young man
could know so much. I sighed,
"What grade did you get?"
You laughed angrily, "C."

I wonder if the professor suspected
you were Indian. And *what an Indian* ...
one of those *exotic* "mixed bloods"
hazel eyes and hair color of sunlight
gleaming red along black tree branch.

Did that bastard professor
ever gave half a thought to why you
may have learned so much about
our already stolen land and what men
like him were practiced at stealing ...
eagles, panthers, passenger pigeons,
frogs, honeybees? A young Indian's heart.

Yes, my brother of the long eye lashes ...
prom king, basketball star, Mohawk Dion
and fancy dancer all the blond cheerleaders
fantasized about in their small town nights.
Dear heart, I can see you kneeling
on the river bank, your tears
the only pure streams left

in those years we lived in the same house
before you started concealing
you are Indian.

Milkweed Ghosts 2013

Along mountain path
milkweed a borderline
between frost-limp fields
and trodden dirt once
an Indian trail ...

milkweed pods split,
silk spilling forth
white as coming snows,
starred with seeds ...
from gray cocoon

burst into dance
so transient, so delicate,
people burst into tears.
Here monarch caterpillars
used to feed on leaves,

weaving their own cocoons.
Here a shudder of stalks
in wind. Butterflies. Indians.
Talk of how they flew free.
Of why they don't come back.

i dreamed of you

last night during the storm

    when I woke at dawn
        dream lingered like snow
glittering to street in a thousand silences

    pale presences   glints

        of snow crystals
swirling like gold moths beneath
    street lamps   frail wings

touching

    down to gutters   cracked

sidewalks

wings of dream moths
        nor'easter mating dance

city street so buried by snow
        i could not stumble my way
back to you

        long time ago
lover

        when i woke this morning
jack frost on windows   ice flower memories

    snow language inside a drift of book

All April Day It Rained

All April Day it rained.
Not just any rain but what people call
a downpour,

downpour
making me think of the poor
and broke down,

inside my shut cracked windows
and half-heated garret
on Binghamton's South Side

remembering the homeless
I spotted yesterday
sprouting like perennial

weeds on the banks
of the Susquehanna,
of the man in black clothes

rumpled and hole-y,
that way he stood with his back
to the river, stared

at road and fast cars
with drivers flush enough
to still afford gas and appear

to be headed somewhere
with the word *home*
gleaming in it ...

All day haunted by the hungry
huddled down and out
along the rising mad rivers

of America, by the red-haired fisherman
I talked to about fishing for walleye
and drinking away pain

while we eyed the ghosts of Indians ...
This April day flooded by old love
in the downpour.

Back to the Blanket

You tell me about nights your old man
stumbled home drunk, you shaking
in bed. When your mother sobbed
Please, don't after he punched
her into screaming walls, you
flung off blankets, flew

to save her. He'd turn then
the firewater fury on you,
sock you in defiant face, twist
flailing arms, make you weep.
Baby. Faggot, he'd sneer. *Son
of a bitch like her, you green-eyed
bastard.* Some nights you leaped

into bed again, wrapped blankets
around bones to soften blow after blow.
*This is why I'll never trust a woman
because when they'd find the bruises
at school my mother would cover
for him, swear he didn't mean it,*

he was drunk. Your words
slam me in my gut, heart.
*I still wrap myself in blankets
on the hottest summer nights
because of his beating me,*
you add, voice a flat line.

Please don't, please don't,
I sob. But no sound comes.
Please trust me, please don't push me

away, please don't hit me into a wall
of rage. For all that you are such
a big Indian, tall, tough, this small

woman finds in you the small boy
of fisted nights. Once, didn't returning
to the blanket mean going back to a past
proud way? Didn't a man and woman
wrap each other in a single star blanket?

Now look at us. Shrouded
in a robe of scars.

How to Get Hired as
an Indian Writer/Professor

Remember what General Sheridan said,
"The only good Indian I ever saw
was a dead one."

Forget about all your publications and awards.
Don't even bother to mention what you do for your tribe
and the whole community of life on Earth.

Stop smiling. Sign of weakness.

Hang yourself. Slit your wrists. Eat, snort, shoot
drugs. Wash them down with firewater. Grow sick
on frybread and other fat-and-sugar sodden foods,
comfort for a few cheap moments.

Make sure you get fucked literally
or metaphorically (pick your poison)
by too many colonial types.

Hey, at least their schools taught you
the definitions of real and un-real.
Of what counts and what is *poetic*.

Of how to fake an orgasm.

So be grateful. They like that ...
an Indian being spiritual.

Don't let on about the tenderness, the beauty,
that once lived in your heart.

Think about it. That's when a University
will hire you, *see* you. When you're dead.

Good and dead.

On Turtle's Back Rising Out
of the Brainwashed Waters

Eating Paul Newman's
    gourmet popcorn
        gilded with Irish butter ...
Except for the cat
    CBS Evening News sole company ...
        Swallowing down salty kernels
with red wine,
    Indian poet food staples ...
        Drumbeats of maize popping
in corn oil, and this old broad still hot
    for Paul's blue blue eyes ...
        sapphire sizzle surviving him ...

Staring at discolored shadows,
    hearing flat line TV voices ...
        more Americans losing jobs,
about to lose jobs,
    unable to get jobs ...
        Wisconsin workers rising up
to save collective bargaining, wages, the unions ...
    rumors Ohio will be next,
        Pennsylvania, Florida ...
maybe the entire country. The world.
    Remember "Cool Hand Luke"?
        Paul-Luke mocking the captain's lines ...

What we have here is a failure
    to communicate ...
        My own defiance trying not
to choke on kernels of anger ...
    sipping the blood wine of lingering hope ...
        Why has it taken us so long?

What happened to *We the People*?
How did they do this ...
that small percentile
of gated faceless oligarchs,
greed wanting to break us until
we are grateful to be slaves?

January in Social Services ...
me with three college degrees ...
body-searched men and women in vast glaring room
staring down and inward
so no one would shame any one
by meeting eyes imploding
towards hopelessness ...
possible homelessness ...
recalling sister-in-law who emailed
We don't want you
and nobody else wants you, either
when I asked to stay

in her and my younger brother's
peachy keen-painted Victorian house
while getting my MFA ...
What makes people think
themselves superior enough
to be that cruel?
Please, mysteries, let me keep my kindness.
Sobbing back then, sobbing
again in my heatless car
when learning how poor
I'd become, desperado
crying over cell phone

to an old lover
who had become a new lover ...
him driving over a hundred miles
to hold me to life

that freeze moon night ...
    While this night high wind warnings
slash in orange over
    February's other dire news ...
        no more blue-eyed popcorn,
winds lashed through with wails
    of America's poor on Turtle's back
        rising.

Uphill

It was War's end, your mother said …
she just eighteen, pushing a carriage uphill
in Catskill town.

You had seen sepia photos of the teenager
your father called "Indian princess"
in censored letters from the Pacific …

model thin dreamer in hand sewn dresses,
cheekbones like those of Hollywood actresses
with back teeth pulled for that "exotic" effect …

your malnourished mother pushing
"hand-me-down" carriage, in lilac shadow
her son born with rickets and bowed legs …

yet she swaying luminous, head held the way
her mother taught her, as she taught you
to walk balancing a book atop your head …

dreaming of the day her Marine husband
returned home after being shot on Guam,
fighting in San Diego hospital to survive.

A rich man gunned his car past your mother,
brayed "Stick your nose up much higher,
someone will stick it up you from behind."

Your proud mother tilted her face up
further towards sky, bearing firstborn away
from hate towards stars. This you remember

each time some coward sticks it to you from behind,
seeing you as that jackass saw your mother ...
poor, vulnerable, undeserving of beauty and pride ...

and you think of your eldest brother, hair
like a snowy owl and joking his bowed
legs are why he's such a great dancer.

Your mother, your brother,
who taught you to dance uphill
with eyes raised to the kind stars.

Pulmonary Embolism

Released from hospital into late
January, you need to walk off
the days and nights in high room
where you stared from hospital bed
at snowless hills above the nervous
city's South Side houses. It all flashes
beautiful after the doctors said you
could have died. But that blood clot
in your lung pained your heart enough
to take you to the ER to be saved.
So you stroll this Sunday sunset past
the neighborhood's foreclosed lives
to Susquehanna and Chenango Rivers ...
on the way home chat with Jewish dreamer
some Lakota people call Little Crazy Horse.
You miss the long ponytail he cut
after his parents died. He explains the gap
between his funky restaurant and discount
liquor store ... paved over earth, metal tables
and black backless benches the politicians lied
would make a park. A professor
in Environmental Studies concluded
the right kind of trees didn't grow there,
so the old bird-shelterers got chain-sawed,
replaced by new young trees
fashionably thin. Little Crazy Horse
and you *get* what it means not to be
the *right kind*, torn up by ancient roots
and rendered song-less. Together
you lament how the politicians
refused to save the old movie house
after the fire. Secretly you recall
seeing your last film there,
"The Magdalene Sisters" ...

making matinee love on scarlet
Victorian couch at theatre's rear,
three nuns down in front,
you and Korean poet lover trying
not to shout "Oh, God" when you
came together under his winter coat
in an un-clotted January
of happy snows.

Blessing Moccasins

She had come back to Binghamton again

All your life
Wanting to see what's over the next hill
And the next hill and the next

Younger brother's words making her laugh
Not quite knowing why they struck her funny

You've always been like that

But then the tears came
And nephew they called "the Gentle Giant"
Hugged her

Don't cry you'll be okay

They were standing out in U-haul back lot
Under a dirty streetlight stars they couldn't see

Jesus I hope you don't move for another ten years

And her brother she once was a little mother to
Also hugged her inside tree branch arms

She began grinning like sunrise
Seeing the next hill

Which a dream had told her
Was a magnificent mountain

Then they drove off
She to latest temporary rooms in Appalachia

One moon later she powwowed up north

Life flamed in the balance
September between summer and fall

In midday light trees glistening
Beneath near white sky leaves tinged gold

She spotted a pair of moccasins
The ones in another dream of hers

Deerskin of palest brown
Flowered with green yellow red beads

My aunt made these

Mohawk woman from Akwesasne watching her cradle
Softness of a deer's life in her hands

Long delicate patience of an elder's stitching
Slow singing hours of beading beauty

Akwesasne woman with face like the day
Eyes flying up above her smiles

Some dreams are worth paying seventy bucks for

Dream moccasins like Mother Earth she is wearing
Bare feet like Sky Woman's they're embracing

Blessing moccasins
Telling her some things go on forever

Ready to dance her over the next hill

Cat & Mouse

I rejoice in the mouse
that got into my cat's food
how my landlord phoned
early this morning
woke me up
so I could give him
the rent check
half asleep because
I was up until 4 am
piecing together my latest
manuscript of poems
Playing Ping Pong in the Nut Ward
while trying to catch that mouse
so after I told him the story
of who ate my cat's food
he shared the sad story
of the mouse who nibbled
a hole in his luggage
to store cat food
now become mouse food
for the coming winter
thank you mouse
for keeping me working
thank you cat
for feeding the mouse
I so terrible at deadlines
thank you best landlord ever
for being my alarm clock
gratitude for your curly hair
for renting me my new life
when I was all tears
I celebrate the poetry
mailed in snowing galaxy
on mouse time

Neighbors

After you left, your downstairs neighbor
moved upstairs to your two story apartment.
Months later when you returned for a visit,
the neighbor mentioned how the quiet man
next door surprised her on Christmas Day
by speaking. He said, "I always thought
your friend was so nice. Her smile made me
happy, like maybe life is worth it."

You and the man never spoke except
for a quick "Hello." *That* and your smile.
He was one of those men a person can't describe
when asked to. Your downstairs neighbor
would joke, "Definitely FBI. Possibly CIA."
Mainly he was a shadow hunching toward
an unseen side door, a strange little man
whose lights flinched on and off late at night.

Then you moved back to that city.
You drove up to your old place, bullshitted
for an hour with your stoned neighbor
who had transformed your former rooms
into something approximating a hippie
garbage dump. Your neighbor lilted,
"Remember the FBI man? Turns out
he had colon cancer. He died last month."

You and she stared out second floor windows,
August sun flaming over hands and house plants
wilting in Dog Day heat. You sat silent as the man
who once passed beneath the windows. Did he ever
want to scream the truth when you smiled his way?

"Look, damn it, I have cancer of the ass. They call it
the silent killer. Please, hug me, hold me, save me
from this silence. I need some human touch, yes, love."

"I feel so bad," you stammered to your once neighbor.
Of course it was one of those stupid clumsy
human things that people say when no words can
ever say it. When a person starts questioning the so-called
social graces or those boundaries the shrinks suggest
their "clients" keep. "Yup," your neighbor smirked,
"That FBI man told me he missed your smile.
He said he really dug your green eyes, too."

Reading the Names 9.11.2011

Today I stood under sky,
violet at dawn then graying
to rain by noon.

I started reading
the names of the dead ...

every Indian who died
in terrorist attacks,
beginning with Columbus.

Thunder cracked nearby
and made me think of the guns.

I remembered the ghosts
beaded with bullet holes,
the ones in canoes

who wave to me
from the Susquehanna.

I prayed they fared okay
in this week's flood and will eat
pancakes once more at Manny's Diner.

I read until twilight mists
silvered in. Raindrops wet

my lips like multiple delicate kisses.
I wondered if ghosts kiss ...
maybe more delicate than this.

When the rain stopped
I watched a star shine out.

The terrorists stole my language
so the names shone out mute.
My heart knew

the dark city was still
in a state of emergency.

Part V

Washington Street, Binghamton

After the poetry reading
a friend drives me around
the corner so I won't have to
walk past State Street bar
where the last stabbing happened,
drops me by my battered car
color of mist twisting up off
Susquehanna.

Tired, I lock my doors,
then hear drumming
on window. A man's face
droops on the other side
like a forgotten flower
pressed thin between the pages
of a Binghamton night,

and I don't even know why
I do it, why I'm not afraid,
maybe just exhaustion,
but I roll down electric
window and smile into
the close hungry face lit
by Van Gogh blue eyes.

"I'm mentally ill," thorazine lips
tremble. "I only get 180 dollars
a month in food stamps. Can you
give me something for a Coke
and hamburger and fries?"

I dig up some stained dollars,
place April fool greenness
on shaking palm. He smiles

"God Bless you," teeth missing,
but I still see the lover
in that face, see a small boy
shine beneath silver hair.

"I'll meet you someday
in Heaven," he lilts. My voice drags,
"We are meeting in Heaven right now,
where our smiles are." "Irish?" he grins.
And we begin singing "O Danny Boy."

Psychobabble-Bubble Moratorium

(Just say "no" to FDA-approved drugs)

Today I am getting in touch with my inner
Masterpiece Theater, declaring myself Queen ...
not just for a day, either (check out 1950s
"Queen for a Day" TV show to see
just how non-poignant and not humble
I plan to be for the rest of my noble life).
Queen Moi doesn't care a wit if twits
like hamsters turning the bubble wheel
of psychobabble label me *delusional*,
dysfunctional, or *trouble coming*
in long flowery skirts and uncut
anti-social indigenous wisdom hair.
I am getting in touch with my inner
medicine woman. I am descended
from a Mohawk medicine woman
and will be bringing the real medicine,
including love medicine, back.

So don't drool your psychobabble
defining of others as *sick* non-words.
Don't run any game trying to make me *sane*
as you see it, turn fabulous me into a pre-fab
cog in your construction material
for an invisible police state letting shrink
pushers prescribe designer tranquilizers,
speed, anti-depressants, you name it,
while The People continue to get arrested
for using the sacred herb and peyote.
Practice *tough love*, establish *boundaries*,
don't *enable* others or be *co-dependant*,
accept that you have *ADD* instead of *HDD*
(Horseshit Deficit Delight). Beware of

dysfunctional people, pretty much
your psychobabble world's entire population.

Yes, be a Smiley Face slave. "Suck it up"
then swallow down legal drugs each morning,
each high noon at the Not OK Corral
and in that endless night you can "go gentle into"
on sleeping pills. This Medicine Woman Queen
is *trouble* and *I am coming.* Just ask my lover
what a big bang my second coming is,
because this tongue doesn't stick itself out
for your drugs whose side effects murder
ecstasy. This tongue is for kissing
and singing. Today Queen-Me is swinging
her tomahawk-scepter, tossing it into
the psychobabble-bubble world ...
pop pop pop pop pop pop! Makes me think
of popcorn, yum. Makes me want to uncork
a thousand champagne bottles, make infinite
toasts to crossing boundaries, being with sweet
human beings all around Earth our Mother.

Here's to celebrating the end of ignoring
why countless men, women, children
weep invisibly behind the walls of America
and where houses once gleamed
in Iraq, Afghanistan, and all countries
of dreams before the invasions.
I decree *No more tough love.* I declare
No more shock, just awe. Today is for
resurrecting that anti-psychobabble word,
Freedom ... for our tongues to slow kiss
wonder and drink love.

Storyville

Jazz blasting out of Bourbon Street bars,
I scrape elbows with hustlers under laced
balconies, brush against singing drunks
brandishing beer bottles, glass glinting
amber in gold New Orleans night air,
sweet papas on the make, pretty mamas
swinging plump hips beneath red hot neon,
vomit stench and stale pee rising up
through gutter grills. Flush

with wine I sway, notice cream-colored
cat slip into loud strip joint where
a creamy whore gleams corpse-like,
ass up nude on wood slab hanging
at a tilt from high ceiling. Unsure
if the woman is real, I trail after
the cat, reflect on marble reflection
swinging above an arena
of male bodies and bottles shining
in elongated mirror.

I stoop to pick cat up, press
burning face into silk fur, knowing
it could be me suspended up there,
a Bellocq photo surviving Storyville.
What woman hasn't imagined being
a whore? The Black man at room's end
spins out blues, Jelly Roll style:
"I got a woman lives right back of the jail,
She got a sign on her window, Pussy for Sale."
I scratch purring cat behind soft ears …
"Nice pussy pussy." Yeah, could be me.

That Day I Sang "Blueberry Hill"

after I heard Fats Domino had been lost during
Hurricane Katrina, belted out "I found my thrill"
while driving to community college to teach afternoon
Comp class. September glowed across usually
sunless Binghamton as light I once felt in NOLA
one long ago fall when I first flew there, fell

in love with Vieux Carré, music of tongues
made soft, hot, sweet, sexy by Cajun food,
musicians playing jazz around every next corner,
octoroon ghosts of Storyville weeping "How beautiful
we were," languorously dancing to saxes, horns, clarinets.
Yes, a New Orleans day in New York State ...

so I took my students outside to read essays
I assigned them about those people trapped
in hard rains, floods, Job's city, so they might
learn through the writing of the mystery of words
the path to inhabiting another person, feel others' sorrow,

only the young man who read first described
a black woman, called her fat, a leech on the system,
lazy, on welfare, an unmarried mother of three
who slopped around all day eating Twinkies.
I felt the city of my own body flooded
by his hate, "No other country in the world
would allow this woman to exist" ...

Shocked faces of Black students, Native students,
Puerto Rican students and all the poor in our circle.
I remembered Martin Luther King, Jr.'s words,
that unless a man was willing to die for what he
believed in he wasn't a man, and I figured King
meant it the same for a woman. I said I could not

tolerate racist remarks, asked that young man
if he were a leech for living off my ancestors' land,
while one of my Black students half-wept he had
relatives in New Orleans, and my Blackfoot student
said he had been homeless once and always gave
what he could to people begging on the streets.
I said, "So do I," remembering that woman
on TV, pleading for help,
hugging her hungry babies.

Then I noticed a Rolex watch glinting
on the racist student's white wrist,
hand fisted to support his punch
of words, spitting at me,
"I think I'll get out of this class,"
and me thinking silently,
"I sure hope this is the last
I see of your arrogant ass."

Later I learned he sprinted
straight to the Department Chair
to complain I was too political.
Yes, I sang "Blueberry Hill" that day
and wasn't rehired that winter to teach
for less than slave pay. But
they found Fats and at Fall's end
my students of color thanked
"Sweet Sue" for making a stand,
sang "You are our hero,"

never knowing that I
drowned in the hurricane.

Song of My I

(*I celebrate myself, and sing myself* ... Walt Whitman)

The coeds of America's elite colleges
inquire about the "I" in my poems ...
Why do you write about yourself? ...
hinting it is bad form to use first person
or mention stories best kept unmentionable,

and I stare at them all product shiny
from vitamins, Trader Joe treats,
crème de la crème schools,
their birthright entitlement
to posh jobs and high pay ...

and I see how they have never
been treated as a "she" or an "it'
struggling to remain silent
because being born poor is
the same as being judged guilty,

how I am like one of those monkeys
the neuroscience students control
with implanted electrodes, "chimp
for a day" so I can afford food
after I perform for chump change

and take this "I" out to a cheap diner
before "star me" drives a hundred
or three hundred miles back to
rented rooms where I sit in shock
with the secret life of plants.

Here

in the cranberry bog
water's edge

White pine protecting her back

Sun searing her face open

Little Bear Medicine Boy
recalling he is wolf
not dog in red collar

She unhooks the leash

Wolf pup splashing into brown bog
chasing water skaters

Water flashing up to blue light

Here remembering something
but she can find no name for it

She has only a few real words left
akwe:kon nya:weh sek:oh

She sheds long skirt blouse muddied shoes

Here

wading naked into the center
lifting jelly cluster of polliwog eggs
from bog deepness

Little Bear Medicine Boy leaping at water's edge
prancing sideways

Wolf dance gold in tree-mirrorings greening to leaf

Here something wordless in hands
slight weight and wobble of it

Something like tiny dead ravens
waiting to be born

Pressing our Feet to Ghost Footprints

The year I heard about Mohawk relatives
my immediate family had somehow lost,
I phoned a couple of the cousins,
both named Pat, and it didn't matter
that we were scattered from Appalachia
to New Jersey to Adirondacks …
once we started talking it was as if
we had grown up together
in our agreements about dreams
and love of woods, rivers, animals and birds.

The two Pats told stories about our ancestress,
medicine woman who found shelter
in Mongaup Creek Valley, drowned
in flooding stream while running medicine
to a sick white boy. They invited
my sister and me to a family reunion
where the woman's house still stood,
and on a Dog Day Sunday we drove
back roads to meet our lost relations.

I do not know how to speak or cry
what genocide and Diaspora have done.
I can only try to write my and my sister's joy
at having a potluck picnic with people
whose Woodlands spirit we recognized,
green blaze at edges of eyes and smiles
welcoming us back to mountain land
long ago grandmother bore children on.

After the picnic, sister and I trailed behind
our wild band of cousins to where creek
barely flowed, like us a mere trickle now,
although its small water snagged the sun and shone.

We pressed bare feet to ancestress' ghost footprints,
posed for each others' cameras in the other
wordlessness of straggling home.

Surprising Gift

That sunset at Methodist retreat Koinonia
        somewhere past Buffalo and Annandale, Minnesota,
you and other Servas travelers gathered to eat
        Chinese "take-out" after board members spent a day
of doing whatever it is that board members do
        while you did what non-board Indian poets do

which earlier in September light
        meant dawdling down from wood shelters
to glacier-dug lake where you collected a lone
        feather, soft grey tipped with white,
then slipped off red knee socks and black suede shoes
        to wade in the holy waters of minnows

and minute snail spirals, sun sparkles flashing you
        back to lover driving your old Toyota
from Bogie Lake, Michigan, across Indiana, Illinois, Wisconsin
        and Minnesota just in time for big sky sunrise
blooming like cosmic wild rose casting
        petals of pinkness across slight land swells

and people still dreaming in the deeps
        of sleep, in the scatterings of towns
and occasional farmhouse
        startling as a feather dropped to earth
in some moment of quick killing ...
        yes, lake-mirrored sun shining you

back to sunrise train whistles plaintive above
        linearities of tracks transporting you further
to yesterday's hundreds of miles
        feeling like centuries of Midwest railroads
forcing out the bison and Indians, leaving
        only place names like Pontiac and Buffalo

to hint of the genocides …
        back to Indiana sand dunes you walked barefoot over,
factories spewing out poison plumes
        on each side of National Park, across Lake Michigan
Chicago in windy haze ... *I've never heard so many train whistles*
        you moaned to lover carrying your shoes

so you could feel free again,
        unburdened as 19th century Blackfoot children
before they started starving and Methodist missionaries
        brought them on trains from Canada to Catskills, children
who never made it home to families after Methodist boarding school
        but married in with New York mountain people …

and after you lamented industry train whistles
        hearing in silence like a lone grey feather
the Chippewa poet who read with you in Grand Forks …
        I hate the sound of trains …
how University of North Dakota voices
        and all car, train and factory sounds ceased

on the wing of her voice rising sadly
        but beautifully above days and nights and centuries
of tragedy and Diaspora into the secret places …
        flashing back to you weeping at a rest stop near Eau Claire,
cold, an abandoned feather, reading brown monument
        outside restrooms three in the morning …

chilling facts about paved land you shivered on,
        roosting place of 136,000,000 passenger pigeons,
all massacred, last pigeon dead in 1914 at Cincinnati Zoo …
        you gazing at the Great Bear as great as you had ever seen her,
rest stop lights and car and truck headlights
        unable to dim the stars of her sky medicine

touching constellation body to highway …
        in Koinonia crumbling apart fortune cookie

at supper for Servas people still imagining roads of peace
on that quarter moon eve of equinox yellows,
in your Blackfoot hand a Chinese word feather
You will receive a surprising gift very soon.

Swims with Frogs, Memorial Day

No one knows what Indians called this river.
It only carries the Dutch name for stream, *kill* …
mated to English *beaver* breeding female sex jokes.

Memorial Day July hot, she walks
to the Beaverkill to swim. These Catskills
are glutted with *kills* …

name conjuring up
extinct panthers who once sleeked
through blue hemlocks' *manitou.*

Before she sees, she hears them …
not panther screams but some music
vibrating soft inside the bright heat.

Nearing sandy beach
she spots tree frogs, hundreds
puffing out pale throats

to create courtship music,
bobbing along water's surface
frogs atop each other …

rainbow colors, myriad sizes …
mating in clear amber above
slippery river rocks,

everybody dumbly happy,
children squealing, kneeling
close to let froggies

make love to hands or feet,
while across the Beaverkill
swallowtail butterflies flash forth

from chrysalides in May trees,
wings small suns glinting
yellow in current sparkles

where she floats among
balloon-throated princes singing
to be kissed out of their skins.

After Washing Her Hair

After washing her hair
naked she sways at mirror,
combing through wet tangles
sprinkling on breasts
while behind her reflection
beyond window
May rain splashes
along old spruces,
Manitou mists embracing
mountains. She foregoes
the looking glass, opens
window to gaze far
beyond this house
her lover bought,
rooms she roams in
like a cat who maybe
will stay, maybe not.
Panther and Indian ghosts
wander in rain bringing Sky
to Earth, lilac bushes
and apple trees bloom
purple, pink, white,
mingling their wayfaring
scents for the golden bees.
When once more the leaves
turn, she will turn
sixty three. Friends
in their eighties laugh at her,
"You're not old!"
Remembering this
she thinks of her man
with his rain-colored hair,
dawn sky of body arched
and pouring into her,

screaming together
like Catskill panthers
she never did believe
were extinct.

Joe the Chief

After we watched the bull buffalo
trot along a herd of cars in Yellowstone,
ranger trying to nudge bison defiance
into pines with white pickup and siren,

we read the sign about Chief Joseph
and other Nez Perce Indians running
like that buffalo among the tourists ...

On a summer night in 1877, hundreds
of "non-treaty" Nez Perce – bands refusing
confinement on a reservation –
camped near here. They journeyed
1,170 miles in their quest for freedom.

On a summer day in 2013
we kept seeing buffalo once said
to be vanishing the way we Indians
were proclaimed to be vanishing.

One shaggy baby buffalo
I wished I could hold in my arms
the way Joseph held his newborn
when his wife, Springtime,
was wounded at Big Hole,

as if such cradling could heal
what happened by Yellowstone River ...
make right the Nez Perce captured 40 miles
into Canada then forced back.

I suppose Joseph's eyes became
like the eyes of Grandfather Buffalo
on the hot park road, wild, befuddled,
sad beyond sorrow ...

that smoke dance of buffalo
making everyone's heart stop
before they took a picture
and drove on.

Peaceful Assembly

After four decades of living away from Catskills,
I moved back to high quiet road where I was born ...
mid-April daffodils yellowing into blossom,
petaled suns confident there would be no more snow.

September now ... morning's mountains
a silver assembly of lingering mists and waning
rain. Wet goldenrod has replaced the daffodils,
first tinge of blood-red edging the maple leaves.

Here is a peaceful assembly, mainly,
except for country men pressing chain saws
into felled trees and the distant highway sounds
of truck wheels ... brakes occasionally squealing.

I have been to those cities where the eight wheelers go,
streets in which I have known other assemblies,
peace marches and sit-ins and silent standing ...
my and others' hope flowering vivid as daffodils.

Yes, I am home in the Manitou Woodlands,
old she-animal moving closer to mingling
worn and scarred body with ancestors' bones,
with ash of my mother who in 1970s

warned how it would become ... *We are*
losing more and more of our freedoms.
The ones being born now won't even know
how much freedom they've lost.

Last year, camping out in Wisconsin's
North Woods, I met a woman who once had
a small farm where she and her family milked cows
by hand. Gone. She described the corporate farms,

cows clamped to steel circles of mechanical milkers
instead of held to the cycles of seasons and fingers
warm like the ones we cradled our wine glasses
and that night's fearful sharing in.

The Rockefellers bought most of the land where I live again.
Orange "Keep Off" signs abound like pre-winter leaves.
Morning mists rise up like bald eagles who also came back …
at blue horizon, sky trying to break free from clouds.

Black Hoodie

Trayvon, the week the jury found
George Zimmerman "Not guilty"
for killing you, I had traveled to Oregon
all the way from Catskills. The morning
of the verdict I hiked into redwood forest
with a man I first met when I was not
much older than you the night you died.
I wanted to walk up to the mountain laurel trail
because I love wild laurel even when it's not
blossoming. Perhaps you had heard of
enchanted forests when you were a little boy …
the redwood forest was like that,
a greening deepness shawled with moss,
the great-girthed trees seeming to touch sky.
The immense agate of forest shimmered
with blues among leaves lit to emerald,
roots rising up like runes over the trail.
Near a surprise of Indian pipes, where
the shiny laurel leaves began to show,
I spotted a black torso beyond my feet.
Yes, a magical forest … I saw you.
But when my heart recovered its beat,
I drew closer and the torso became
a black hoodie just my size. I knelt
to pull the fallen blackness on, warmly
soft the way your skin must have felt
the evening your heart lost its bountiful
beat. I always did hate Florida's gated
communities like above ground graves
for the living dead. Trayvon Martin,
I wish you had found an enchanted forest
that would have protected you from being
hunted down. I wish you could have
happily eaten millions of Skittles, traveled

and found a woman who loved your skin
and you as a starry night. After emerging
from redwoods, my old sweetheart and I
heard the verdict on NPR. What runes
or blues can grow back the beauty
of a seventeen year old boy-man cut down?
I shall wear the black hoodie until I die.

Swimming in Quinault Lake

On your 64th birthday I am remembering
summer's cross-country journey to
black scorpion deserts, mesas, L.A.
north to Olympic Peninsula rainforest,
swirling mists like Manitou mists
of Catskills where we now dwell,

wondering if my many ancestresses
mated with nomads like you
unable to stay still when over the next
hill might be a place like Northwest
transformed by coastal rains into
enchantments of lush ferns, moss,

cloud-touching cedars and mystery mists
glazing Earth's greens to dream shine,
to a place like Quinault Lake where we
camped after watching July sunset,
sky rambling rose and wanderlust purple,
so tired we only stared into a brief fire

before flaming into binary star sleep
of primordial man/woman returned
from fishing, berry picking and wandering
out into the wonder of an evolved world,
at sunrise you surprising me
with campfire coffee to lure

my body awake and back to lake
sacred to Quinault Indians, where
we swam within a hoop of misty
mountains, out of the dawn
waters I a salmon leaping
towards you so male beautiful

in an ancient wild and unkempt way,
in intensifying light through fog
droplets of water sunbursts in your
silvery hair and unruly beard,
eyes with Mongolian cast to them
smiling up at horizon line.

Stone Sculptor, Snow Moon Dream

I would tell you about my mother
the way we once woke up
spoke our dreams during Catskill sunrises

of hungry years after my father died at 51
mother's hair silvering in sorrow
mica schist in dawn light

about her eyes grey like yours
      grey of stones glimmering under river water
      grey of stones flaming with eagles on blinding cliffs
      grey of stones glowing back to stars
            in the tongue-less nightlands

I could whisper my mother's chant
      This is a dream all a dream

      drifting into garnet silences

So last night this dream with its pretense of some solid "I"
this conglomerate of first stardust swan turtle muskrat
      grey sea and greening island

dreaming of you after your stone sculptor's voice
gleamed through red phone
      glint of laughter at voice edge

after re-hearing the day you smiled you were shy
me not looking at you then only at your sculptures
      condolences of birds bears deer white pine vision faces

grateful to you because of my own shyness that hides
      inside a crazy quilt of joking words

You at powwows Indian festivals
　　　Seneca Cayuga dreamer man
　　　　　explaining to strangers in voice reticent as soapstone

I try to find the spirit in a rock bring that out

Last night you came floating towards me
in fire opal light

as if in invisible Stone Canoe
as if The Peacemaker arrowing towards
　　　my sleeper's heart

Heart flint since my mother died
　　　　　others died

Last night
　　　your hair mica schist
　　　face quartz crystal
　　　eyes wolf eyes circling moonstones

You gliding into the clay of my sleep
ancient shyness
　　　quasar buried in bedrock

Grey Eyes, this dream in human form doesn't crave explanations

Enough to wake this winter's dawn
　　　as in the old Catskill days
　　　as in a fossil of peace

Scarf of Many Colors

Today a country girl trilled
up at me as I was gathering eggs
in the last aisle of Peck's grocery,
"Oh, I love your scarf with all
the many colors in it!"

I smiled "Thanks," told her
about my long ago student, Kat,
who knitted the scarf, gift for me
that Xmas ... how that scarf
knitted our friendship. Girl lilted

"It is just so pretty, so pretty,
those soft rainbow colors."
This sounds like such a simple
exchange, a brief encounter.
Big deal, you might say.

But the girl and her chant
chiming like a bird's song
reminded me of other Catskill girls,
including myself when I was eight
or nine, sweet in that way

only a mountain girl will be,
in proudly washed but frayed dress
and barn sale coat chosen for its
vividness, and the innocence of eyes
before someone steals their awe.

Yes, girls here don't talk,
they sing like birds that fly and
swoop around in forests and out into
the sleeping fields, helping us dream
our way through winter moons ...

those magical bird girls
who open doors for old women,
who open hearts to old memories,
like this January thaw
knitting a day of many colors.

Mitochondrial DNA Love Medicine Mama

When you bring what appears like one body
to what seems to be my only body, skin
to skin until we begin losing boundaries
in blaze of touch, please know

it isn't Deer Cloud you flame into
but all the women who glimmer
in my Mitochondrial DNA …
mothers glistening back to

First Woman who sparked
double helix dance expressed by long
hair, eyes of many colors, freckle
constellations, and tongue, lips,

smiles luring you to where
ancestress love medicine
bewitches your loins.
Know, my dear, that I come

out of Africa, and after that
the dreamers who became me
migrated nearly everywhere …
Selkie isles, Ukraine, Mongolia,

and America where they lay with
shape-shifting Indians. When you
make love to *this* seal, bear, fox, bird,
prepare for a trip around the world,

for time-travel back to rambling
mamas who explain why I was born
a starburst of wanderlust, wake
each day to a sunrise of wonder.

So where to tonight, my darling?
Morocco, Wales, Turkey, Belarus, Bohemia?
Come, I give you all the languages of love.
Come-cry with me all the words for Goddess.

Bios

Poet Susan Deer Cloud is a mixed lineage Catskill Mountain Indian who has returned to her "heart country" to live once again with foxes, black bears, bald eagles, great blue herons, and the ghosts of panthers and ancestors. An alumna of Goddard College (MFA) and Binghamton University (B.A. & M.A.), she is the recipient of a National Endowment for the Arts Literature Fellowship, two New York State Foundation for the Arts Poetry Fellowships, an Elizabeth George Foundation Grant and a Chenango County Council for the Arts Individual Artist Grant. Published in numerous literary journals and anthologies, some of her other books are *Braiding Starlight, Car Stealer, The Last Ceremony* & *Fox Mountain*. For more, you can write to her at susan.poetrymatters@gmail.com, visit her website at http://sites.google.com/site/susandeercloud/ or greet her among the sacred hoop stars and Manitou dawn mists.

Artist Dorothy Little Sparrow Watson, Cherokee, is a retired Art Teacher. Self taught, she likes vivid, wild and evocative colors and uses them widely in her paintings. She has lived in several countries and thinks she has picked up some of her ways of art through the different colorful cultures she has dwelled in. She still tries to find the time for her Art whenever she can. She has many secret paintings that are still waiting to come out of the closet. She considers Susan Deer Cloud to be a dear friend/sister of hers and is honored to have done the watercolor for *Hunger Moon's* front cover.

www.ingramcontent.com/pod-product-compliance
Lightning Source LLC
LaVergne TN
LVHW091256080426
835510LV00007B/287